THE BIGGEST MARTIAL ARTS LESSON OF ALL

VOLUME ONE
ORIGINS

Including sections on:

The Origins of the Martial Arts
Kenpo
Taekwondo
Martial Arts Equipment
Karate
Kang Duk Won

QUALITY PRESS

For complete information on Matrixing the Martial Arts,
go to: MonsterMartialArts.com

ISBN-13: 978-1974437771

ISBN-10: 1974437779

TABLE OF CONTENTS

The Most Polite Man in the World Did Kwon Bup Karate
The Obsession with False Martial Arts Power
Real Karate Does Not Look Like Karate!
Things Wrong With Classical Karate Training
The Three Distractions that Stop One from Reaching
        the True Martial Art.
Three Types of Martial Arts Styles When It Comes to Work Outs
The Great $2 Karate Lesson!

ABOUT THE BIGGEST MARTIAL ARTS LESSON OF ALL

Al Case walked into his first Martial Arts Dojo in 1967. Since then he has studied countless martial arts, written for the martial arts magazine (with a column, 'Case Histories,' in Inside Karate), written dozens of MA training manuals, produced hundreds of hours of Martial Art videos, owned and operated a dozen Martial Arts schools.

And, of course, he is the 'inventor' of Matrixing Technology, the only Martial Arts science on the planet.

This ten volume Series, 'The Biggest Martial Arts Lesson of All,' represents the teachings of more than 50 years in the martial arts.

Odd bits of history, how to make techniques work, where Matrixing came from and how to make it work, tips on making perfect forms, the secrets of energy (chi power), little known martial arts, and on and on and on.

More than 1300 pages of arcane bits of knowledge that you will find nowhere else, and that will make you the best martial artist you can be.

For it is true: knowledge is power.

Following are the major sections of the ten volumes. For lists of the article titles within these books see the individual books themselves.

VOLUME ONE
Kenpo
Taekwondo
Martial Arts Equipment
Karate
Kang Duk Won

VOLUME TWO
Stances
Punches
Kicks

VOLUME THREE

Author's Introduction to
The Biggest Martial Arts Lesson of All

In this ten volume series I give you what I have learned over a 50 year time period.

While the individual articles were often written far apart, I have arranged them in an order that mirrors, somewhat, my progress in the martial arts.

Origins, when I walked into Kenpo, the progression to Karate...and other arts.

A thorough analysis of what Chi Power is, eliminating mysticism, replacing mysticism with science, and making your path that much easier. A whole lifetime laid out for you to inspect.

That said, talk is cheap.

I recommend doing the arts I speak of here.

You do not need to do them all, delving into each for ten years at a time, for the science of Matrixing makes the learning process very easier, much more streamlined.

Go to MonsterMartialArts.com. The arts I speak of here are detailed in video.

It would be easy to go through all of my videos, though there are quite a few, in a couple of years time.

You could honestly say, then, that you have 50 years knowledge, and that knowledge would be backed up by your own experience, your own verification that the things I speak of in this book, and in other books I have written, are true.

The Martial Arts are a fantastic path, rich with lore, ripe with physical excellence, presenting a pathway through the mind to the spirit that is unparalleled.

Please don't waste your chance here.

Take my knowledge. Stand on my shoulders.

Heck, jump up and down on my shoulders, and see what you will see. Go where you will go.

Have a great work out!

Al Case

ORIGINS

Where Did the Martial Arts Come From?

I was working in a factory many years ago, and word got around that I was training in the martial arts. A Philippine co-worker came up to me one day, and he said, "No study martial arts, martial Arts bad...bad, " then he shook his head and walked away. From this odd beginning I discovered where the martial arts really came from.

As one might expect, I was intrigued by my co-workers attitude, the Philippines were renowned for their martial arts, and so I tracked him down and questioned him further. "Why are the martial arts bad?" I asked him. This is the story he told me.

"One day I decide I learn martial arts, so I go outside and hit tree. I chop like so (he did a vertical chop, as if chopping down on somebody's forehead), and a I chop and I chop. I chop two hour a day for two year.

"One night my neighbor have wild party, and three in morning I go ask him to stop it. He laughed at me, so I use karate on him. I chop his head and he turn upside down, so I run home and worry I kill him...that why Karate bad!"

I didn't laugh, because he was serious, he really thought the art was bad, and didn't understand that his unique ways of self training, and his own lack of control, might have something to do with 'being bad.' But his tale led me to wonder where the martial arts came from. I mean, they are the world's second oldest profession, so where did they come from?

They came into being because somebody wanted to take something away from somebody, and they came from somebody wanting to stop somebody from taking something away from him. This is the same as lawyerism, but applied to the actual hit and punch that occurs when politics breaks down. Eventually, the idea of taking something away from somebody, or protecting your property from somebody reached the levels of armies and weapons of mass destruction.

The idea that what you have belongs to me, and I don't have to pay you no stinkin' money...that is where the martial arts came from. And people train to war, and steal money and property and wives and whatever else they covet. And, oddly, as my previous words indicate, the solution to this avarice and misbegotten art is...in the study of the true art.

You study the art to protect yourself, and in that study you discover yourself...you discover your self worth, and the idea that you are honorable and don't have to fear others, or that they might take from you. On the day that everybody on earth knows the martial arts, on that day the avarice and war stop, and on that day everybody will know where the martial arts come from. They come from within, from the spirit that is you, from the honor that motivates every beat of your heart and every breath you take.

Were the Martial Arts Really Born this Way?

Joe Blow goes to war, rolls in the mud a lot, manages to survive, and he comes out of the wars with a couple of techniques that worked, that actually saved his life. Maybe pushing the butt of his spear for a horse impalement, maybe ducking when somebody sliced sideways at his head, maybe stepping to the side if they sliced down, and, oh, BTW, stick quick after the other guy misses.

So Joe Blow survives, gets a bunch or ribbons, which are a lot cheaper than a pension, and is pronounced a hero.

Unfortunately, when poor Joe goes home he doesn't have any way of making money.

But the kids in his village are all impressed, and they keep asking him stupid questions like, "How did you survive the battle of Bloody Gap?"

Which battle he survived by being conked on the head and sleeping through it, then waking up in time for the general to come by and think he's the last man standing. That was good for a really big, red ribbon.

But kids keep asking and asking, and, finally, in a moment of frustration, he throws a bozo kid on the ground, sticks his knife right to the kid's throat, and says, "Like this!"

Now, the kid, being stupid, doesn't realize that he's pushed Joe to the breaking point, he is just aware that he has sampled all the violence and glory that he missed out on. And he gets up and says, "Wow! Can you teach me that?"

Disgusted, Joe walks away and throws back, "You don't have enough money to buy that technique!"

"I got ten dollars!"

Joe stops.

He's broke, he's hungry all the time, and this stupid kid wants to pay him ten dollars because....because...

"Okay!"

So he teaches the kid the technique. Stupid kid actually nicks him with a knife, so he grabs a stick, tells the kid everybody trains with sticks.

The kid asks why not real weapons, and Joe makes up some gobbledegook about sticks being wood, and wood is mystical, therefore the stick is mystical.

"Wow! Am I learning the Stick Mystical System?"

Moaning on the inside with grief, Joe says, "Sure. Call it 'Stick-My-Sys-Do.'"

Kid goes away all excited, tells his friends, and the next day Joe has 14 brats squalling to learn Stick-My-Sys-Do.

Joe's eyes light up like a cash register, and he teaches the kids. But when they complain about being thrown on their butt he sells them pillows to put in their pants. Protective gear, you know.

So Joe teaches his five techniques, and then realizes that he has no more! But those kids have been paying for his beans and brewski, so...so he remembers a guy in the wars who told him about how you roll under the charging horse and slash the belly with a knife. Guy was making it up, but what would a bunch of stupid kids know? Eh?

So he teaches them the mystical and sacred technique Rolling Horse Undies.

Then he figures, he got away with that one, he makes one up. 'Punch Under the Horse's Tale.'

Which are quickly followed up by Kicking the Cocos, One Finger Up the Nose, and all sorts of other things.

And if any of the kids get mouthy, or give him a rough time, he just uses one of his real techniques to throw the kid on his, uh, pillow, and stick his knife (he's allowed to use a real one) in the kid's throat.

And everybody cheers and yells and wants to learn more.

Now, I know, you think I am bitter and cynical, or even (choke) disrespectful. But, if you have a better idea, feel free to share.

This has been an official Case History. You can read more like this at Monster Martial Arts in the column menu. And if you want to learn some real martial arts, not just Rolling Horse Undies or Punch Under the horse's Tale, check out this sacred and mystical page that nobody has ever seen until you saw it.

The Reality Of True Martial Arts

The Secret of the Martial Arts is how to achieve Awareness. The Secret of All Life is how to achieve Awareness. Thus, the Secret of Life is within you, and all you have to do is figure out how to grow awareness.

This is such an easy thing, so simple, and yet people overlook it. People think that they will be better martial artists if they just work out more, build their bodies, can beat up the other fellow. Nothing could be further from the truth; this is actually diametrically opposed to the truth of themselves as martial artists.

Yes, muscles should be used and grown, but only to a certain degree. They are important only to the degree that they enable one to make themselves aware. One should work the body to make it larger and stronger, but use it to achieve awareness of what the muscles are and are doing.

Yes, forms are important, but only to the degree they enhance awareness. As one does forms one becomes aware of how to move the body. Eventually, with correct practice, one will transcend the normal ways of moving the body and discover whole new concepts of motion.

Yes, martial arts applications are important, but only to the degree that they bring awareness of how to deal with the problems presented by an attacker. One discovers, through martial arts techniques, that the real problem has to do with analyzing and handling incoming forces. This makes one into a more aware being.

Yes, freestyle is important; the combative disciplines wouldn't be real if they weren't combat ready. However, the big problem is that people start to love combat for the sake of combat, and not as a method for becoming more aware of how to use the body...even under stress. This is called the Joy of Combat, and is contrary to the real path of the true martial art.

The real key is that one should be learning the martial arts as a discipline to explore ones own self. When one loves combat more than learning they are not learning the art. When one engages in combat to beat the other person, they will never uncover the true spirit of themselves.

The eastern combat disciplines are a key, and the whole body is the lock. Do the martial arts and unlock the bodies true potential. Still the mind and discover the spirit that is the truth of you.

Head over over on Monster Martial Arts and pick up a free book if you want to learn more about the True Martial Arts.

To Learn Martial Arts There Are Three Things You need To Know

To learn the martial arts you need to learn three distinct things. You will find these things in every legitimate martial art. If you don't, then the fighting discipline you are studying may not be a real art.

The first thing to be learned are forms. There are people who look down on forms, deride them as mere dances, and that sort of thing. The truth of the matter, however, is that forms contain all the tricks and techniques, and they provide a learning platform which not only leads one to learn how to fight, but far beyond.

To do a form requires a stable stance, and that is the moving platform you will be using to deliver powerful self defense techniques. By doing martial arts forms you will learn how to relax, and learn how that relaxation creates power. Lastly, every time you do a form you are strengthening your body, even as you practice fighting techniques.

The second thing to be learned has to do with the self defense techniques themselves. Self defense tricks teach one how to move the body, how to set up for action, how to stay calm in the middle of the fight. The thing to remember is that every time you do a self defense technique you are doing a miniature kata.

Now, techniques aren't totally street oriented, and one will have to tweak them slightly should one have to use them in a street fight. However, the classical power you have developed by working on techniques will come out in your street defenses. Your punches and kicks will draw on that classical martial arts power you have been practicing.

The third thing to be learned is freestyle, and this is where it all comes together. This is where you get to try to use the classical moves, or at least tap into that classical power in a controlled setting. Remember, freestyle training is as close as you can get to street self defense as possible.

When freestyling you must learn how to control yourself and not hurt your opponent, and yet build the ability to inflict great damage should you wish. This is a difficult thing to learn, but it is at the heart of the oriental disciplines. Anybody can learn to fight, you see, but only a real artist can learn how to control himself in the middle of a fight.

In closing, one can learn how to fight easily, but that is not the point of it all. What is important is to test yourself, strive to expand yourself, and learn how not to be a fighting animal, but a human being with great powers on tap. This is the real reason one should learn Martial Arts.

KENPO

Back in the Beginning of Kenpo…

I began studying Kenpo in 1967.
It was so unknown that it was called Kenpo Karate so it could be
identified with the art of Karate. Not that that many people knew what
karate was.

Kenpo was born in Japan. There are many lineages, but the specific
Kenpo that is so widely known these days came from James Mitose,
Thunderbolt Chow, Ed Parker, and finally, an instructor near you.

Martial Arts were not studied widely at the time, and usually it was
fellows who were tough, who looked forward to the street fight, who
studied them.

Kenpo came from Okinawan Karate and Japanese Jujitsu. There were
other sourcss, many and varied, but the American style Kenpo you might
study was likely based, at least in the beginning, on these arts.

Right from the outset Americans realized that Kenpo could be marketed
more easily through tournaments, so we studied our freestyle rabidly, and
we looked forward to the weekend trips.

For such a violent art, the participants at these tournaments proved to be
a polite bunch. Schools were located a distance apart and there wasn't
much competition. Instructors actually looked forward to seeing each
other, to comparing notes, and even learning a 'secret' technique or two.

And, outside of school, fights did happen. Proud warriors, Kenpo stylists,
all martial artists, were happy to step up to a challenge, take umbrage at a
veiled insult, trade fists with a goon.

We were more rabid back then. We didn't do ten or twenty kicks and
think we were done, we would do a couple of hundred and chide

ourselves for being lazy. We would do forms by the hour. See if we could do 60 forms in an hour.

In short, we would exhaust ourselves. We would go for a run, do some weightlifting, and then freestyle for a couple of hours in class, and know that we were doing it right.

Mistakes? We made a ton of them. But over time we fixed them; the martial arts tend to be self fixing; the turn of the foot, the line of the wrist, the physics of the universe corrected us and were our teachers.

And now, near fifty years later, all we wish is one thing: to do it all again. To do Karate and Kenpo, to throw and kick and punch to our hearts content.

And we feel sorry for all those people who quit early, or who were born too late, or who were just too lax in their training to really find the truth: You are what you do, that is your measure, and that is your worth.

If you want a REALLY good book on Kenpo, consider 'How to Create Kenpo' by Al Case. It has the real history, the one you don't hear much about, plus a section on how to do forms, plus 150 kenpo techniques, thoroughly analyzed so that you can be the best Kenpoka you can be. That's How to Create Kenpo, available on Amazon. The hard work is up to you.

Here's a fascinating bit of history: The Man Who Killed Kenpo. (website)

Hey Mate! What's Yer Kenpo System?

Maybe you remember that great scene in Enter the Dragon where the bad guy asks 'What's yer style' of Bruce Lee? As over the top as that statement appears, it points up the differences of arts, and how confusing such a thing as lineage can be. In no art is this as true as in the art of Kenpo.

Many people think Ed Parker created the style of Kenpo, but he actually only popularized it. And, to be honest, he more than likely added to the confusion of the art. He created something like five different versions, and he drew from Karate and Kung Fu and whatever happened to be on his mind that day.

Kenpo got its start in Japan. There is some confusion as to the correct spelling, some people saying Kenpo, and some saying Kempo. Kenpo usually refers to martial arts stemming from China, and Kempo refers to the more Japanese oriented arts.

There is confusion on this point as there is not agreement. Further, there is not always common lineage. That said, Kenpo, although believed to mean 'Fist Law,' is actually 'Quanfa,' which means Kung Fu.

The main types of the Kenpo in the USA come from James Mitose. Master Mitose is sometimes a controversial teacher, for he was tried and convicted of murder and extortion. He served his time in Folsom Prison.

Mr. Mitose taught William Chow, who taught Ed Parker. Mr. Parker, as has been described, popularized the art of Kenpo. Students of Mr. Chow include Adriano Emperado, Ralph Castro, Sam Kuaho, and others.

Names of the arts taught by these people include Shaolin Kenpo, Kajukenpo, American Kenpo, Kara-Ho Kempo, and many other types of the art. There is an abundance of secondary students who were taught by these people. Kenpo has also continued to grow conceptually, drawing from many other arts for kata, self defense applications, and so on.

Though Kenpo grew at a tremendous pace, and though the lineage is sometimes difficult to follow, as is the art itself, there is much value in it. Many people 'wet their feet' in the convenient 'Strip Mall Dojos,' and then continue their studies elsewhere. Still, to define the true system of kenpo, and to list the roots and influences that resulted in that art can be a daunting task.

Matrix Kung Fu...Monkey Boxing, simplifies and condenses Chinese Kenpo Karate. Head on over over to Monster Martial Arts and make sure you pick up a free book while you're there.

The Things That Went Wrong With American Kenpo Karate

I walked into my first American Kenpo Karate dojo back in 1967. This was the Rod Martin variation of Tracys Kenpo, which was an offshoot of Ed Parker Kenpo Karate. Therein is the first problem with American Kenpo.

It grew too fast. In the orient teachers didn't teach until they had a minimum of a decade of experience, had studied under a variety of teachers and had learned a variety of martial arts styles. We were borning senseis every three years, which is how long it took to make a black belt back then.

Of course, there is also the problem of which kenpo is the true kenpo? Ed Parker, you see, developed five different kenpos. If you learned an earlier version, is it now considered...less than kenpo?

And, this bring us to the fact that there are variations on the variations. There are people who have evolved combat kenpo and tournament kenpo and MMA kenpo, and so on. It seems there are as many kenpos as there are people studying it.

I first became aware of this problem, too many variations, while putting together Monkey Boxing, which, in one sense, is my version of kenpo, or at least as close as I can come to a kenpo. I had studied the version of a version of it way back when, then I picked up Larry Tatum Kenpo, and I had some of the kenpo connection material, then I came across rather massive instruction manuals on Olympic kenpo, and I believe I had two other versions of the art.

As I went through the endless techniques I saw how the changes were sometimes small, and sometimes large, but always unique to the person making the changes. Now, to be sure, every art should be an expression of the individual, and kenpo does seem suited to this. Still, it would be nice to have a specific set of concepts, and maybe a list of techniques that would standardize the kenpo field before individual martial arts masters expanded it with their own variations.

In the end, I boiled the techniques of five complete arts, with a couple or three partial arts, down to forty techniques. I am sure there will be some who shake their heads at this. After all, how can one summate over 500 techniques, and all the evolutions thereof, with but 40 techniques?

Well, I offer no excuse, I merely invite you to try your own hand at collecting sufficient variations that you might have a complete overview of the art. Then, start organizing the data. It will be difficult, definitely a number nine headache, but you might find yourself a true master of American Kenpo Karate.

Al Case, the greatest martial arts writer of all time (nearly 2 million words in print), is at Monster Martial Arts. You can examine his 40 technique version of American Kenpo Karate there. Make sure you pick up his free ebook on Matrixing.

Kenpo History Sort of a Mess

Kenpo Karate is one of the most popular martial arts in the world, and the history is, to put it lightly, a mess.

There are three men who brought Kenpo to the streets of America. These are James Mitose, William 'Thunderbolt Chow, and Ed Parker.

James Mitose learned the art at a temple in Japan. Except, there is no temple there. The area is the home of kosho sect of the Yoshida clan, so maybe. Except...when you think about it, would there be much significance if your instructor learned Karate at a Baptist church somewhere in Illinois?

Yes, there are differences in culture, and there is a potential zen aspect to it all, but churches are basically meeting places.

The second man in this lineage is William 'Thunderbolt' Chow. Professor Chow claimed that he originally learned martial arts from his father, a Buddhist priest. Except, there are no records of his father as a priest. And how does that tie in with the Kenpo he learned from James Mitose?

The third man in this saga is Edmund Parker.

Parker brought Karate to the mainland, began teaching martial arts while at Brigham Young University. Except, he is said to have taught his students all he knew - he was only a brown belt - and when he went home and tried to get more to teach...Professor Chow wouldn't teach him anything because he had been instructing without permission!

Now, there are a lot more sordid details to this story. There are fights and arguments and people slandering one another, and the reader might think, at this point, the this writer is writing black headlines just to sell an article. Except...the real problem here is not the three men, it is the students learning their kenpo karate martial art.

People seem to need to bolster themselves up, to give themselves airs, to make themselves sound more important than they are.

So when Mitose says, in an offhanded remark, 'Yes, my father used to show me tricks when I was a kid. We were living next to a church then, and we would roll around on the grass in the side yard. Lot of fun...' the student bows deep and realizes that his instructor studied at a zen temple, was beaten with a bamboo rod for dozing, and had to go through rigamarole that would make Gordon Liu envious.

And when Thunderbolt Chow says, 'Yes, my father had dreams of being a priest, talked about it often. Priests know really great martial arts, you know,' the student holds his finger aloft as the lightening strikes him, and knows that he studying ancient and arcane mysteries written down in scrolls dating back to the time of Buddha.

And when Parker says, 'My instructor didn't have any more to teach me,' the student catches his breath and claps his hands together, for obviously his instructor has surpassed his instructor, and the student is the real beneficiary of all this light and goodness.

Yes, there are people who spread rumor and prevarication to make themselves look good, but it is up to the student to be discerning and find out the real truth...and, there is a lesson to be learned here.

The lesson is that man learns best from his mistakes. He learns a little bit from doing something well, but he learns A LOT from messing up. And these three men, James Mitose, William 'Thunderbolt' Chow, and Ed Parker, they were human, and they messed up.

So, are we going to make them saints and pretend they made no mistakes? Or are we going to look extra hard at their mistakes and learn, truly learn, from them?

The author began studying Kenpo Karate in 1967. He has written a perspective of Kenpo called 'How to Create Kenpo.' In that volume offers a unique perspective of Kenpo.

The Five Kenpos of Ed Parker

The first Kenpo of Ed Parker was actually Okinawan Karate. One can see the forms in the string of techniques in his first book. Forms were actually not taught, except, I believe, for Naihanchi and maybe one or two others.

The second version was a blend of Karate and jujitsu. This version was originally taught in a small temple in Japan.

The third Kenpo of Mr. Parker was actually created by James Wing Woo, a kung Fu stylist who taught Ed's class, and helped him write a book while he lived in Pasadena. This was the version of kenpo from which many of the forms were originated.

The fourth kenpo was a reworking and renaming of the 3rd version.

The fifth and final Kenpo was created by Ed Parker to replace the earlier styles of Kenpo. He was proud of the fact that it actually wasn't kenpo anymore.

Now, this all stated, one has to ask why there were so many styles. The answer is simple, Ed was trying to simplify and make sense out of the mess.

The fact of the matter is that the martial arts are random sequences of motions. This causes the art to be hard to learn, and hard to apply. It is simply hard to memorize to the point of intuition so much data.

Ed was trying to simplify and make sense out of the thing so that students could learn faster (among other reasons).

Unfortunately, he failed.

He came close, but his efforts were still comprised of random sequences of motion.

Each method he designed or compiled or whatever was built upon the ashes of the previous, tried to include new concepts and theories he had come across, and does not make summation of kenpo, or the martial arts.

Was he wrong for doing what he did? Not at all. His work was ground breaking and innovative, he just lacked the logic and perspective to bring it all together.

Does it mean that the kenpo you are studying is wrong?

Nope.

For Kenpo is a manifestation of knowledge, and each person contains the knowledge in his own unique way.

Though Ed failed to make the art a science, it is still an art, and it is still whatever people make it.

From Ed Parker Chinese Kenpo Karate to Matrix Kenpo Karate!

That Kenpo is broken is obvious. Actually, not to hurt anybody's feelings, it has been broken from the get go. One simple proof is that the founder himself, Edmund Parker, presented five different versions of the art during his lifetime.

Five different versions, starting with a shotokan karate based version, and progressing through a variety of made up kung fu. Yet, before you decide I am nothing but a detractor, all the martial arts can be found in Parker's Kenpo. It is a massive system, and the potential is unlimited.

Now, the problem is that most kung fu systems have been passed along for generations. They have had hundreds, even thousands, of years to become developed, polished and evolved. Chinese Kenpo, on the other hand, has not been benefitted by this process.

The first version, the classical karate version, was extremely workable. Parker ran into difficulties with his instructor, however, and ran out of material to teach. Thus, he hired a kung fu artist from the San Francisco area, Jimmy Wu, to help him put together more material.

The next four versions of Chinese Kenpo, then, are they Parker? Or are they Wu? To be honest, they are probably a mix, but of what percentage?

And, to be fair, one must realize that Parker, through his lineage, and Wu, through his, did bring a certain amount of tried and tested material to the board. And, one must realize that the times were rich with material. There were all sorts of systems of karate and kung fu making their appearance, and Parker had front seat through these times.

That brings us to the intent promised by the title of this article, how to fix Kenpo. The best way to fix Parker's Kenpo is to throw away the rankings, categorize the techniques by attack, and arrange them in order of difficulty. While this has been done somewhat, in doing it anew one will find all sorts of things that were left out, over emphasized, and so on.

The point is that all the martial arts are there, but they need to be arranged in a more workable manner, and only by a more scientific analysis is one going to come to grips with the truth of Kenpo. When I did this I came up with a system I called Monkey Boxing. Though, to honest, one could call the system Matrix Kenpo Karate.

The Terrible Truth About Ed Parker

I've heard many stories of many arts that were, shall we say, less than honorable. The one I heard about Kenpo Karate, however, is one of the worst I have heard. Unfortunately, I don't know how true it is, but with the data I present in this article perhaps some one could let me know if they have any light to shed on the truth or falsity of it.

Ed Parker is credited with being the founder of modern Kenpo, putting on the biggest tournament in the world for years, the Internationals, teaching movie stars, including Elvis, and all manner of other deeds. His prowess is quite well known, and his students are legion. Unfortunately, when he first began teaching, while he seemed to demonstrate a talent as a teacher, he was only a brown belt.

In those days he was actually teaching the Heian forms from Shotokan karate, this as illustrated by one of his earliest books. Running out of material to teach his students, he returned to Hawaii and was told to go take a hike, the founder of the system apparently had lost interest in him as a student. I'm not sure, exactly, what the fall out was, but it was perhaps that Ed was teaching without permission.

Ed then ran into a fellow in San Francisco named Jimmy Woo, whose named might have been Jimmy Wu, who knew tremendous and authentic gung fu, but who spoke almost no English. Ed brought Jimmy to Los Angeles, where they lived together, and where Jimmy created the Kenpo forms, the techniques, and so on. Ed took these forms and techniques and began teaching them as his own.

To complicate matters, Ed asked Jimmy to write a book with him on what they were doing, and Jimmy spent his days writing kenpo, teaching Ed and some of his students, all while still being deficient in the English language. One day Jimmy saw a rough translation/draft of the book that Ed was planning on turning over to a publisher, and he was surprised to see that his name was not on the cover, or anywhere in the book. This was surprising, because even though Ed was half the team, Jimmy was doing all the work.

Why not my name on book, is what he was supposed to have said. Ed said he would explain, but he had an errand to run, could they take a drive, and Ed would explain on the way. Jimmy hopped into the car, and Ed drove into Hollywood, but Ed didn't say a word about the book the whole time he was driving. On Hollywood Blvd, there is an Armenian pastry shop there now, Ed let Jimmy out of the car, and drove off.

Jimmy had one single quarter in his pocket, the clothes on his back, and nothing else. With that last quarter he called one of Ed's students, who he had been teaching. In his broken English he explained what Ed had done, that he didn't know where he was, or why it had all happened.

He had been teaching, writing, and suddenly, he had been betrayed. Now, is this story true, or is it a pack of lies? If anybody has definite facts, I sure would like to know.

Ed Parker and Bruce Lee were Traitors to the Martial Arts!

I always enjoy saying that people like Ed Parker and Bruce Lee were bad guys in the martial arts. People always get upset with me and talk trash. Then, when I tell them the truth, they are left with egg on their face.

Ed Parker apparently never made it to Black Belt in the system taught by Thunderbolt Chow. Heck, halfway through teaching his students, he had to go home to Hawaii because he ran out of material and needed more. And, Chow told him no.

So he made up stuff, hired a kung fu artist to help make up new forms and techniques, restructured his system (five times), and so on. The result was that he could award tenth degree black belts, hold tournaments, start chains of schools, and word has it that he was only a brown belt. And the whole world was fooled into thinking that he was the grand poobah of martial arts, and hardly anybody but a dedicated Kenpoist knows who his instructor was.

And if you think Ed Parker was bad, wait until you consider Bruce Lee! Word has it that Bruce 'The Little Dragon' Lee didn't finish his Wing Chun training. He was apparently involved in the street gangs of Kong Kong, and his parents finally had enough of his bad ways and sent him to cool off in America! In America, though he hadn't completed his Ving Tsun training, he started teaching that martial art openly.

Not knowing the whole Ving Tsun system, he began augmenting it with studies in boxing, fencing, and 24 other martial arts. Yes, he was a sponge, but he was a gung fu teacher outside his community, betraying his race (according to some), and teaching stuff that went beyond the classical and accepted arts. He was teaching a wild eclectic system that went far beyond the forms training of the time.

The culmination was a fight with no winner (Wong Jack Man), and then he throws it all away for Hollywood! Is that the mark of a true martial artist? Or is that some unbalanced fellow whining for fame?

Now, it is time for this writer to fess up. Most of you readers know what I am doing anyway. I am engaging in a little yellow journalism for sarcastic sake.

Ed Parker, Bruce Lee, and other pioneers studied sufficient in the classical to know what it was, then they chose, for whatever reasons, their own directions. They then outshone their teachers and systems, and expanded the martial arts to the benefit of all. Yes, Bruce Lee and Ed Parker were traitors, as are all true visionaries, as need to be anybody who wants to go beyond stiff training methods and learn the truth of the martial arts.

Want to be a pioneer in the martial arts? Want to develop your own style and discover the truths that Bruce Lee and Ed Parker discovered? Come on over to Monster Martial Arts.

How To Make Power Kenpo!

You can make your system of Kenpo into Power Kenpo fairly easily. Of course, you're going to have to go against the old school boys, but this isn't always bad. In fact, if you do make your system into a Power Kenpo system, you will be following the footsteps of Ed Parker more closely than the old school boys.

The concept of Power Kenpo is something I coined many decades ago, and have never really talked about. It actually grew from an incident in 1968 in which I asked my instructor to take a look at a form I had been working on. My instructor stepped on to the mat and I took a position and began to move.

The form was actually out of a series of books on Japanese Karate, and it is called Heian Five. It is a strong form, with solid stance and large, significant movements. As such, it seems to stand opposed to the fast whirling arms of Parker Kenpo theory.

I finished the form, and my instructor observed, "Yes, definitely a Japanese form." He didn't say much more, and I had the feeling that he was displeased. Many decades later, I understand the displeasure, he was trying to teach me one thing, and I was straying in an entirely different direction.

To be honest, Kenpo Karate does not fit well with classical Shotokan Karate. Kenpo, as I have intimated, relies on fast hands and circling motions. Shotokan holds a disdain for subterfuge, and preaches the power of a strong stance, facing your enemy squarely, and attacking in a linear manner.

Each system has its strengths, and its weaknesses, but they don't fit together. It is difficult even to shift from one art to another in the middle of combat. The funny thing about all this is that original Kenpo was built upon the Heian forms of classical Karate.

Most people blink when I say such a thing, but it is true. If you can find a copy of one of Ed Parker's first books you will find that it is nothing more than a sequence of the applications of the Heian forms. Indeed, if you link the applications in his book, you are actually doing the Heians.

In conclusion, now you understand what I mean when I remarked about Power Kenpo and being true to the footsteps of Ed Parker. The fact is that true and dedicated martial artists should study as many systems as they can. The truth of the matter is that if you want power in your Kenpo, or accelerated weapons, or better kicks, then study a separate system that has what you want, and let the power of that other art bleed back to your kenpo, and that is how you will have Power Kenpo.

TAEKWONDO

The History of Taekwondo is Long and Glorious

The history of Taekwondo is generally assumed to be short, merely back the forties. This, in fact, is not so. The history of Taekwondo stretches not just through the millennium, but through arts imported into Korea.

A couple of thousand years ago, when Korea was still divided into three kingdoms, young men were selected for special training in warfare. This training consisted of all aspects of military training, including archery, equestrian sports, combat strategy, and so on. These men were the cream of the crop, selected because of their high athletic and mental abilities.

These young warriors were called the Hwarang, and they specialized in a martial art called Subak. The various styles of Subak were combined to give high training in footwork and fistwork. The most popular of the Subak arts was called taekkyeon.

During the middle ages martial arts training waned. This was because of the Chinese influence, especially that of Confucianism. The thrust of society was more towards manners, and the practice of the martial arts was more confined to backyards.

Then came World War Two and the Japanese occupation. The Japanese were dedicated to destroying anything resembling Korean culture, and any traces of Taekyyeon or Subak were ruthlessly stamped out. While this was cruel and oppressive, there was a bright side, for the Japanese brought their own martial arts with them.

Koreans embraced the hard core principles of Karate joyously. The martial arts flowered, and were represented by nine Kwans, or houses. Eventually, after the war, the nine kwans were brought together under the Taekwondo name.

Still, the Koreans wanted their own cultural identity, and the Japenese forms, and even the accompanying Chinese influences, were pushed aside in favor of new forms. These new forms, though lacking in power, were easier to teach, and taekwondo began to be exported to the rest of the world. Currently, Taekwondo is one of the most popular martial arts in the world, being taught in over 123 countries with over 30 million practitioners.

The final phase in this history of Taekwondo is now occurring. Koreans are beginning to search for the power of their original arts, and even looking into the heavy duty influences of the Japanese influenced kwans. Ultimately, the Korean martial art of taekwondo will reabsorb the power of the japanese forms, the heady concepts of the Chinese arts, and yet forge a link with the original Subak arts taught so long ago.

The Hellish Beginnings Of Tae Kwon Do

Many people walk to the corner mall, walk into their Korean Martial Arts dojo, and train in nice, neat uniforms, watching themselves in wall sized mirrors, hit bags in between sips of their designer water, and think that they are doing the die hard Tae Kwon Do. What these people should know is some of the history of Korean Karate, and particularly of Korean Karate. They will find that that polite kick punch combination they are practicing was born in hell, perfected in hades, and then things got nasty.

Just to let you know, this article is speaking of the history of the kwans from Korea of the fifties. This includes the nine major kwans, which are sung Moo Kwan, Chung Du Kwan, Moo Duk Kwan, Chang Moo Kwan, Yun Moo Kwan, Han Moo Kwan, Oh Do Kwan, Kang Duk Won, Jung Do Kwan. There are other Kwans, and schools that grew from these nine, but these nine are the main ones.

Korea is a rugged, little peninsula, about half the size of California, jutting from the Asian continent. It is a land constructed half of plains, and half of rugged, eternal mountains. It experiences extremes of siberian cold, stifling heat, and monsoon rains.

Throughout its history, Korea has been embroiled in countless wars. The Japanese held sway during the first half of the last century, and in the early fifties Korea became the battleground between the free world and communist forces. Thus, this small bit of land came under the boot heel of million man armies, and the people were in constant flight, or killed outright.

The communist forces attacked first, causing a mass exodus the length of the peninsula. Peasants were made part of the vast communist army, given no weapons, and put into massive meat grinder attacks. If the peasants survived the exodus, or being forced to fight, they had to endure a winter with temperatures often at 30 degrees below zero.

Those that managed to survive the winters, and the spring offensive of the United Nations armies, continued with their study of the martial arts. That's right, during all the death and disease, in spite of the weather and starvation, the nine kwans survived. Indeed, they thrived.

One tale that made me shake my head in awe of these incredible warriors was that, when the war front approached, the students would pick up the boards of their dojos and head south. That's right, they didn't even nail the boards down, because they knew they would have to flee, and they perfected their spinning, jumping kicks on unsecured, splintered, weathered boards. Got a splinter up your foot...pick it out and keep going, because that's the martial arts.

So enjoy your matts and mirrors, and sip your designer water in appreciation. That Tae Kwon Do you are practicing was forged by supermen, and it is a legacy dripping with blood and sweat and hardship. And when you bow...bow extra low, your ancestors deserve it.

Extreme Martial Arts That Are Real
and Brutal and Hard Beyond Belief

Extreme Martial Arts are a top Google search these days. People, especially those interested in MMA training, are going outside the traditional martial arts academy to learn martial arts training methods that are ever more brutal.

The funny thing is that if they studied their history, immersed themselves in the classical martial arts, they would find all the brutality they would ever want.

If you want extreme martial arts you need look no further than taekwondo some sixty tears ago. I am speaking, of course, of the early taekwoondo--Classical Karate, actually-- taught in Kwans during the Korean War.

To begin with, Korea is a brutal place. Cold sweeps down from Siberia and the Arctic, monsoons sweep across the peninsular country, and during the summer their is blood boiling heat.

Add to that, a war, and you have the most brutal conditions possible for learning your basic self defense.

Imagine standing on a dojo floor. It is built of rough planks that are filled with splinters, and you have bare feet. There is no heater, and you must rely on body movement to stay warm. Then, of course, you have the sound of distant gunfire.

'Pinan Five!' the martial arts instructor yells over the din of approaching shell bursts.

Students move fast enough to stay warm in near freezing weather.

'But Sensei,' asks one of the younger students, one who has just begun this extreme martial arts training and who doesn't know better. 'The shells are getting closer! Shouldn't we be leaving?'

There are snickers through the class, and the Instructor asks for quiet. Then he turns to the younger student. 'We are a hard target, and those shell bursts aren't even a mile away. When they get to a half mile, then we leave. Now, take your mind off the coming death by concentrating on your forms!'

And, when the front is a half mile off, the old instructor tells the students to lift up the floorboards and leave.

Lift up the floorboards?

Yes. There was a shortage of all materials, and a dojo floor, even one rough cut and filled with splinters, is of extreme worth.

Dutifully, the students put on their shoes (snow filled from sitting on the front stoop) and carry the floor of the dojo away. They will hide it, and when the fighting has moved on, they will reassembled and learn martial arts again.

Now, as I said, people are looking for more extreme martial arts. They want fitness and self defense, and they tend to look towards Mixed Martial Arts Training methods, and to forget classical martial arts like Kung Fu and Taekwondo and karate.

But beyond the extreme martial arts youtube supplies and the octagon brings, there are the movements honed during war most violent and brutal. Remember that, the next time you put on the pads and drink the designer water' remember, the next time you want something that makes hard the body even as it uplifts the spirit; remember, even as you merely sweat what only feels like blood and guts.

There is a huge difference between fighting for gold and glory, and between fighting for one's life, and this is the core of extreme martial arts training that makes up the classical styles of today.

Outlaw Karate is a wonderful example of an extreme martial art that remembers the brutality of its beginnings.

The Truth about the Progression of Real Taekwondo Styles

Taekwondo styles are interesting things, as they are each a slice of the whole art, and even resemble the ultimate arrangement of all arts. I say this as a student of one of the original schools of the art, the Kang Duk Won. For the past forty years I've watched as each style of Korea's most famous art has come forth, and there is an evolution of art occurring here.

First, the original kwans, the Song Moo Kwan, Moo Duk Kwan, Kwon Bop, and all the others, were predominately Karate. Most of the fellows who put these arts together studied with Gichin Funakoshi during the forties. The rest studied with his students or asssociates.

Thus, the first kwans were karate, plain and simple. Korea gaining independence, however, and undergoing the throws of nationalism, taekwondo was invented by General Choi Hong Hi. Thus, much of karate was thrown out, altered, and taekwondo began its various evolutions.

Now, there are several styles of Taekwondo, and several evolutions of forms. Most of them are interpretations of simple karate basics, with emphasis on kicking. One should not hold one art over the other, and such things as my Taekwondo is the Deadliest Martial Art, or my Taekwondo is the Best Martial Art shouldn't be bothered with. The individual arts are slices of the pie, and the diligent student will study all the styles, be able to do all the forms, and decide for himself which are best.

That said, one should move into studying the art of Hapkido. Hapkido is a put together by a fellow who studied Daito ryu Aiki jujitsu. There is some confusion on the exact history of the founder, but the art is proving out. It is lasting, and people are learning, but one does need to go into a study of it with open eyes.

After Hapkido there are the original Korean Martial Arts. These would be such arts as Taekgyeon and Subak. Taekgyeon, and there is some variation on this spelling, eventually translated into Hwarangdo. While Hwarangdo borrowed the name, there does seem to be some meat to the art.

Subak is one of the original arts taught before the Japanese outlawed Korean martial arts. It is a delight of drilling and training and throwing an attacker effortlessly. Unfortunately, it may be difficult to find an instructor, but this is still an art worth looking into.

So, the recommendation is that one start off with the simple versions of Choi Hong Hi, and travel through the various groups and systems to find what is best for you. After that, one should explore basic karate, to see the origins of TKD, and then begin a sojourn through Hapkido, and Hwarangdo, and, if one is lucky, the original Subak. While this suggestion of study may seem lengthy, it is the only way to get to the truth concerning Real Taekwondo Styles.

Al Case studied the Kang Duk Won back in the seventies, and it was in its original form. Drop by his site if you want to pick up an absolutely Free Karate Book.

People Have Suffered For You In The Taekwondo Martial Arts

If you have a tendency to be late, or even miss taekwondo classes, consider this little tale of one of the founders of Kang Duk Won Kwon Bup.

Korea is a tough little finger jutting out of the Asian continent. It endures winters that sweep down from the arctic, monsoons that blast in from the Pacific, and summers so hot they make Hell jealous. Into this mix, in 1920, Yoon Byung In was born.

Though his family had once been comfortable, with the Japanese occupation they fell on hard times. Though they were not rich, Yoon Byung In presented himself well, always polite, very strong, and extremely smart. If ever forced to fight, he never let anger rule him, he never tried to deliberately hurt his opponent, but rather fought only to the point of stopping the fight.

One winter, while crouching at a street fire, he fell forward and burned his right hand severely. As a result he lost half the length of his fingers, and wore white gloves from that time on.

During his early years Yoon Byung In picked up an interest in the martial arts. He applied for admission to a Chinese kung fu academy, but was turned away. Not to be stopped, he spied in the windows until the master was chased away. Realizing that he had to prove himself, Yoon Byung In arranged the shoes of the students neatly on the steps of the school every day. The Master of the school finally recognized him, and accepted him as a student.

Graduating from upper school, Yoon Byung In was chosen to go to Japan to study at a University. This was an honor which should have gone to an elder son, and which showed just how smart and hard working Yoon Byung in was.

To continue his martial arts training, Yoon Byung In took to striking a tree on the campus every day. The tree actually started to lean over from the daily bashing. One day a fellow Korean ran up to Yoon. Several Japanese Karate students were in pursuit. The Korean had apparently decided that having a girlfriend was more important than studying Karate, and now asked Yoon Byun In to rescue him.

Yoon Byung In asserted himself, and managed to defeat the karate students, but did not harm any of them. As a result, he met the grandmaster Toyama Kanken of the Karate school.

Toyama Kanken was the first person to open a karate school in Japan, he was a classmate of Gichin Funakoshi, and had studied under nearly all the Okinawan legends of Karate. He was quite impressed with Yoon Byun In, and they agreed to teach each other their systems.

Yoon eventually became the captain of the university karate club, and was promoted to fourth dan.

In 1950 the North Koreans invaded South Korea, and Yoon returned to his country. During this time he was essential, perhaps even crucial, in introducing Korean Karate to his country. Many of his students went on to start their own organizations.

Yoon was asked to teach karate to the Imperial Palace Bodyguards. He turned down the position because he would have to salute, and he was embarrassed about his injured hand.

During the war, Yoon's older brother forced Yoon to go with him to North Korea. Yoon was then drafted and forced to fight in the war.

Yoon was eventually captured and taken to a POW camp on an island off the coast of Southern Korea. When the war ended the allies asked for

South Koreans to step forth, that they would be allowed to return to their country. The North Koreans restrained Yoon and wouldn't allow him to return to South Korea.

In North Korea Yoon was given the task of teaching a martial arts class to the army. His methods and results apparently didn't agree with the party beliefs, and Yoon was relieved of his teaching position and forced to work in a cement factory.

Many years later, suffering from lung cancer (doubtless form his forced labor in the cement factory) Yoon was allowed to return to his home and family.

Broke, this legend of karate passed away. He had scaled the greatest heights, achieved the pinnacle of martial arts, shared his knowledge freely, and then been forced into slavery and ill health.

Consider this the next time you slip on that pretty uniform, sip a little designer water, step out onto that mat surrounded by wall length mirrors, and do your forms.

And be grateful for people like Yoon Byung In. People who suffered war and deprivation, and yet passed on the arts which lead to the establishment of arts like Kukkiwon Korean Martial Arts.

If you want to experience real martial arts, as designed and taught by people like Yoon Byung In, check out Evolution of an Art at Monster Martial Arts.

The Sad and Tragic End of Yoon Byung In

Yoon Bying In wanted to study kung fu in the worst possible way, yet the kung fu master in his town refused to teach Koreans. Time after time Yoon had been caught peeking in windows and had been chased away from the dojo. Then Yoon got a brilliant idea.

During class he snuck up and lined up all the shoes of the students. He then retreated and watched when the master of kung fu came out of the dojo. The kung fu master was pleased at this display of respect, and he wondered who had shown him such respect.

Yoon continued doing this day after day, and, eventually, the kung fu master found out who it was. In this way Yoon became accepted, and the only Korean so accepted to study kung fu in this town. He threw himself into his studies and proved bright and strong in many ways.

Yoon grew older and went to college. He like to practice his kung fu on a tree, and he pounded on the tree so mercilessly that the tree eventually began to bend over. One day a fellow student came running up to him.

We are both Korean, and you must help me. Those Japanese karate students are after me. At that moment a band of the karate students came charging up.

Yoon put himself in the way and told the students that the martial arts should be studied for peaceful purposes. Immediately, the students challenged him and began trying to fight him. Using his kung fu Yoon dodged and darted and managed to avoid combat without hurting anybody.

The karate master heard of Yoon, and became friends with him. Eventually, Yoon went to study with Toyama Kanken, who had studied with Ankoh Itosu. Toyama was so impressed he traded knowledge with

Yoon, and made him Shihan in his system, which Yoon taught upon his return to Korea.

Yoon contributed greatly to Karate, causing the founding of the Kang Duk Won and contributing to the fund of knowledge which became Tae Kwon Do. Eventually he was swept up by the Korean war, where he became a prisoner of war and was forced to work in a cement factory. It is rumored that he never returned home, yet his contributions will always be embedded in the DNA of Karate.

The Truth is that Taekwondo is Really Karate!

Interesting statement, but it is true: Taekwondo came from Karate. Consider the history of the five Kwans.

Chung Do Kwan (Blue Wave School) was begun in 1944 by Won Kuk Lee. Won Kuk Lee studied Shotokan Karate with Gichin Funakoshi, and he used the same forms and called his school Tang Soo Do.

Moo Duk Kwan was started in 1945 by Hwang Kee. Kee actually studied tai chi chuan, then studied with Won Kuk Lee, but he claims he learned the shotokan forms that he taught from Funakoshi's book.

Song Moo Kwan was begun in 1944 by Byung Jick Ro. He studied shotokan, and called his school Tang Soo do.

Kwon Bop Bu/Chang Moo Kwan was begin in 1947 by Byung In Joon. Joon studied Karate with Kanken Toyama, who was a classmate of Gichin Funakoshi.

Yun Moo Kwan was founded in 1946 by Kyung Suk Lee (judo) and Sang Sup Chun (Karate). While this school was original judo and Karate, after the Korean War it began teaching Shito Ryu Karate.

These were the top five schools, and they were all Karate based. The lesser six schools were all derived from these original five.

Comes the question, how did Karate become Taekwondo?

The answer is that Korea is a very nationalistic country, and politics plays a large part. Thus, Gen. Choi Hong Hi decided to bring all the schools under one banner, and to call them by the generic term Taekwondo (Way of the hand and Foot).

Thus, some of the schools still teach the old forms from Karate, and some teach later forms. There were actually a couple of evolutions of these later forms, and so there is confusion in Taekwondo because of this.

Interestingly, probably the school with the greatest claim to being pure Taekwondo would be The Kang Duk Won. This is because the style is based upon the teachings of Kanken Toyama. This kept the system more of a pure link to Okinawa, the birthplace of Karate, and away from the Japanese influence. Japanese Karate is good, but it has been altered to fit certain cultural facets of Japan.

Interested in learning the system that came through Kanken Toyama? Go to MonsterMartialArts.com and look for Evolution of an Art. Evolution of an Art contains three complete styles of Karate, from inception to interesting and extreme variations.

MARTIAL ARTS EQUIPMENT

New Technology Destroys the Martial Arts!

I saw the beginning of this some forty years ago while studying Chinese Kenpo Karate, and it is still going on. In fact, it is worse than ever, and infects the majority of arts. I will give you a couple of examples, and hopefully you can fix your martial art.

I was studying Ed Parker Kenpo Karate, and we began using pads. At first, the pads were only used to help fellows with knee problems, or that sort of thing, but the assortment of pads quickly grew. Soon pads were used on the shins for bruises, on the feet, on the shins, on the elbows and wrists, and so on.

Suddenly, somebody figured out that there was money to be made. School owners realized that selling pads increased the income, and began pushing them to every student for every class. The selling of padding became a million dollar business that infected every school.

Now, you might be wondering why this is so bad. We're just protecting little Johnny, right? But this is part of the school owner propaganda, and part of the selling gimmick.

When you wear pads you think your punches don't hurt as much, and so you begin punching harder. Thus, the protective gear actually encourages more violence, and less control. When you think about it, if you have to be aware and responsible so that you don't get hurt, you start to learn the true art.

The true martial art has to do with control, you see. If you learn how to control yourself, then you start learning about yourself, and this makes you a better person, in and out of the ring. If you think you have to hit harder to be more effective, then the people you fight are going to be more at risk when they fight with you.

Now, I saw this type of thought spread throughout the martial arts world in tournaments. I also saw the introduction of softer (plastic) weapons, so that people wouldn't get hurt, which also decreases the need for control, and for the true appreciation of one's own potential. And, now people must wear cups, chest protectors, mouthpieces, and whatever else they can be scared or forced into buying.

The people who invented the martial arts, who passed them down for millennium, did not use such devices, and I suspect they would have laughed at them. Bear in mind that I am not asking people to get hurt, I am asking that people study martial arts with no accoutrements, so that they can take responsibility for what they do, and not be cushioned against learning about themselves. Whether you study Ed Parker Kenpo, Hapkido, classical Karate, or whatever, you should follow Ed Parker's advice…'I come to you with empty hands.'

Martial Arts Equipment Needs to Be Eliminated

I was there when the first martial arts equipment appeared in the dojos of America. I strapped on the brand new protective pads the Martial Arts gear pushers had brought over, and I experienced the difference between reality and martial arts protective gear.

The first thing we students noted was that the stuff didn't work. In fact, the karate pads we strapped to our shins and forearms and feet and hands and bodies caused heavier impact. In actual fact, we began to accumulate more injuries. Guys were bruising heavily, and there were even a couple of breaks.

The reason for this is simple, when you hit a guy with Karate pads on his forearms or rib cage you think it isn't going to hurt, so you hit harder. This offsets the pad effect, and the result is heavier impact and injuries.

In addition, there is a false sense of security, and the person being hit doesn't make his body as tight upon impact. This undercuts the whole effect of having Martial Arts gear, but, more important, it undercuts the purpose of the martial arts!

The martial arts, you see, teach one control. But once you put on martial arts equipment that is protective in nature, you are taking away the need for control, or at least lessening it.

The point to be made here is that Martial Arts equipment, including shin pads and forearm pads and all the other martial arts gear that is protective in nature, should be eliminated. People should be made to understand what a block or punch feels like, how it has the potential for hurt, and then they will immediately begin to learn control.

I know that what I have said here goes against the common belief, and I know there will be parents and martial arts supply house that take objection to this. Parents, however, are ill informed and need to be educated. The martial arts equipment pushers are making money, so their objections should be ignored.

Now, to be sure, I realize that there may be certain exceptions to this. Wrapping an injury may be useful to protecting that injury from further trauma. And I know that a fellow with injured knees, or some such, should possibly wear something to shore up the knees.

These exceptions are rare, however, and the best martial arts instructors are going to be helping students with exercises that will strengthen weaknesses before they put that student out on the dojo floor for a little karate kumite, or whatever your brand of martial arts freestyle.

The point of this article is simple: if we eliminate martial arts equipment, and demand better instruction, we will have less injuries, and not more, and the Martial Arts will be pushed to higher levels.

The Best Kicking Bag for a Heavy Bag Workout

One of the most fun things you can do, be it martial arts, kickboxing, or just plain on your own conditioning, is a heavy bag workout.

There is nothing like setting, and whomping that sucker with all your might! Whether you do a heavy bag workout for beginners, women, for weight loss or whatever, there is a satisfaction that comes with watching that bad boy fly to the ceiling!

Now, the trick is to have the best bag you can. You have to select a weight that is right for you, and a texture, and so on.

Hard core martial artists will claim that you have to kick something as heavy as an attacker, maybe a couple hundred pounds. The problem is that the bag doesn't have enough give for you, especially in the beginning. Simply, you kick it, and it doesn't move that much, and you don't get satisfaction, and the muscles don't get that feeling of having pushed something.

Now, we don't want a speed bag, like boxers use. That's too light, and the muscles don't get the feel of resistance necessary for weightlifting.

And it is weightlifting, be it fast and violent, and you need to find the exact weight that will work for you.

A 70 pound bag is perfect. It has give, and it weighs enough that it will fly away, but still last you for a while as your muscles get stronger and stronger.

The next step would be a hundred pound kicking bag. After that, you play it by ear, but a 20 to 25 pound increase is about all you want at one time.

No, it doesn't weigh as much as an opponent, but you need to raise the level of resistance in accordance with how your body grows, not form an unworkable ideal right off the bat.

Now, a couple of interesting facts, and then I will tell you where I get my kicking bags.

Before he died, Bruce Lee ordered a bag that was 300 or 400 pounds. He weighed 135 pounds, and I have no idea how much fly he was expecting to get out of that bag, but...man! If anybody could do it, it was Bruce.

And, did you know that kicking bags are stuffed with clothes? True. I think a lot of them have furniture filling, but it was clothes for years for many.

And, the way they fill heavy bags is with baseball bats. They just have a couple of guys pile drive the end of the bat into the top of the bag until everything is squooshed down, weighs the right amount, and doesn't have any...edges.

Anyway, think about what I said here, before you buy anything for your heavy bag workout.

And, if you want to know how I pack my personal bags - yes, I do it all myself - then go to cheap punching bag. The story of how I discovered my method, and the things I went through...it's quite interesting, and it will help you on your journey to the best heavy bag workout you can have. Pick up some free martial arts book while you're there.

The Greatest Training Device in the Martial Arts Isn't So Great!

I'm going to tell you something that you have never considered. The old guys, a hundred years ago, they didn't know what they looked like. They had no means of self inspecting their forms to make they were right.

Odd, eh? But it's true. Back a hundred years ago, especially in some of the third world countries that the martial arts flourished in, they didn't have mirrors.

Nowadays we walk into training halls with mirrors covering the walls. We do our forms, and we inspect our movements, and we know what we look like. Sometimes this is good, sometimes this is bad, but at least we can see ourselves.

The good is that we can adjust our forms. We can see our postural mistakes. The bad...well, let me explain.

There is this thing called narcissism. Falling in love with yourself...and the image of yourself. But image often doesn't have anything to do with workability.

The martial arts rely on energy that is not always visible to the eye, and in using mirrors we start looking at our glorious form, and neglect to create the energy that the form, without obsessing on one's self image, can create. We are not always able to perceive the depth to which we should sink our weight into the ground. We are not always able to perceive whether the tan tien is glowing and growing, and being used the way it should.

A punch should not be a polite line of turning fist, it should be a belly busting explosion of weight and emotion and the hell with the world! A block should not be a wave of flesh and bone, it should be a staunch stance with world shaking focus! A kick should not be the ability to do the splits vertical, it should be a sinking of the weight, a balance while tremendous energies are coursed through the leg and into the foot and...beyond.

A mirror is a great thing, it can impart a myriad of detail, and make us look incredibly pretty, but it doesn't always generate the energy it takes to win a fight. Looking good might be great for evolution into video and hollywood, but it has limited value when it comes to the true martial arts. In the martial arts one must give up the image of self to find The True Art.

The Hard Fist of Karate Training
Makes for an Incredibly Powerful Punch!

When it comes down to hard core self defense, a hard fist is especially desired. Of course, how does one get a fist hard enough to make for a powerful punch? The answer is through good, hard Karate training.

Karate is the martial art Mas Oyama studied when he killed bulls, and his hands were reputed to be as hard as stones. Add to that the legends of the old Okinawan Karate Sensei who could twist raw bamboo apart and you really have something. And, the tales of the old Karate Masters who could punch right through the body armor of the Japanese Samurai, are icing on the cake!

Currently, karate training methods prefer makiwara training. This is a plank, tapering towards the top, that is buried in the ground. While punching the Makiwara has good effect, it does not return one to the training methods of old.

Punching a tapered two by four, you see, can only be done so long, and then the fists start to turn red and ugly and to bruise up. Fifty punches per arm per day is just not enough to make the rock solid fist that we are looking for. No, we need to look a little deeper, go a little more mad dog to find our perfect punch.

Oddly, the method we used in my karate school, and this was over forty years ago, before Karate had a chance to be 'watered down' by commercialism, tournaments, protective gear, and that sort of thing, didn't actually involve the use of the fist. It didn't use the fist, especially as in bashing, but rather used the fingers. Make the fingers solid, and you have a solid hand.

We started out with a simple push up. These are good for the whole body, and they work the punching muscles directly. Then we started changing our push ups.

We would do push ups on our palms, then our fists, then our half fists, and finally our fingertips. This was hard as it didn't require just muscle, but an awareness of muscle. Eventually, reaching one single, outstretched finger, our awareness was what had grown, and our awareness is what made for unstoppable punches.

One single, outstretched finger. Not a finger and a thumb, not a bent finger, but a digit straight as a rod. And, our awareness became as straight as a rod...and unbending as steel. This is the type of Karate training I recommend for people who want the hard fist needed for the strongest punch.

Using Karate Techniques To Break Bricks
Without Breaking Your Hands!

Using Karate Techniques, which are the same as Hapkido techniques or gung fu techniques, it is incredibly easy to break bricks. I'm not going to say that your grandma could do it, or a child, but you could. Heck, a little work and practice, the ability to decipher the sacred words I am about to impart, and you could be smashing the holy heck out of sun dried rectangular blocks.

Now, there was a fellow went to the orient, and he knew martial arts, and orientals loving their back yard barbecues, and even a few beers (pretty American, those orientals) everybody laughing and joking, and they asked this American to break a few bricks for them. You breakee bricks! We have good time!

So the American chopped a brick and the brick sat and stared at him and he near broke his hand. Those wacky tailgate orientals, you see, had baked an iron rod into the brick. Oh, ha ha ha...isn't that funny?

Well, actually, it is pretty funny. I tell ya, those orientals keep it up and they'll be downright American! The point here is...don't break what you don't know about, select your material to be smashed with care.

This subject of picking your material is pretty important. People who break big stacks of ice, for instance, neglect to tell you that the ice has been pre-broken and stuck back together, which makes the ice easy to break. That tends to bend the game.

And, the people who break stacks of bricks or boards often do so by placing spacers between the bricks or boards, which, again, makes the bricks or boards pretty easy to break. Have them break the bricks and boards without spacers, and you are seeing a real power break. And, yes, your humble author can break five one inch pine boards, that's five inches of wood, with no stinkin' sissy spacers.

When you pick a brick to break, pick a dry one, dry ones are easier to break. If you want your ten year old cousin, or your grandma to break a brick, cook it in an oven for an hour or two. And, it helps it you set the brick with one end on the ground and the other end on another brick, and drop the end of the brick as your hand hits the brick, this increases the sharpness of impact and makes the break that much easier. Now, those are the tricks, except for the specificsthemselves.

When you break a brick have your hand loosey goosey, and slam it down, and tighten it upon impact. This will focus your energy and protect your hands, and I have seen these principles in virtually all martial arts. Korean Karate techniques, Shaolin techniques, Kwon Bup techniques, Kenpo techniques, they are all based on the same principles, and these principles define how easy it can be to break bricks.

Karate Breaking Technique Applied to a Man's Skull!

Karate Breaking Techniques were the rage back in 1967. This was because Karate, and other martial arts like Kung Fu and Taekwondo were new to the land. Nobody knew anything back then, and darn, if you could break a board...why, you could break a man's skull!

There are some interesting things about a skull, and let me preface this article on karate breaking methods with a rather fascinating datum.

While a skull is hard and rigid, it is easy to break. To prove this take an egg out of your refrigerator, hold it in your palm, and...without using the fingers!...squeeze.

As hard as you squeeze, that egg is going to laugh at you.

Now, use your fingers, and clean up the gooey mess. If you squeeze a skull it ain't gonna break. If you poke it soft enough, it will. How soft? Fifteen pounds of pressure per square inch is enough to break a skull.

There are a lot of variables, of course. The skull bone differs in thickness. Hair cushions. And so on. Which puts the real force required somewhere between 16 and 196 pounds. Hit a fellow in the side of the skull, right behind and above the eyes, and the bone is thin, and it might take only 15 pounds of pressure to break that puppy. But thee are some places where the bone is thick and the pressure could take 200 pounds easy.

But, that said, a karate strike, properly done, will range from 300 to 400 pounds of pressure. That should be more than enough to crack up a skull.

So what stops a skull from being cracked when a karate punch is applied to it?

First, a skull in motion is harder to break than a skull in place.

A karate punch will frequently glance off a head moving frantically out of the way. In other words, you have to have the intended target hold still so that a perfect karate strike can be focused exactly if you wish to increase your breaking chances.

Second, speaking of moving out of the way, if a surface is pliable it will resist breaking much more than a surface that is rigid. This is to say that a skull being karate kicked will move back, thus dissipating force; which is to say that if you want to do your karate breaking techniques on a human style head, it would be nice if that skull would lay down on a concrete surface with no give.

And, speaking of karate breaking techniques, we come to the juice of this martial arts article. If you want to break a cranium, you need to practice your martial arts breaking techniques on similar objects first.

Start with Karate board breaking.

To build your break a board technique, start with one board. Number two pine, an inch thick, 12 by 12.

Once successful, go to two boards, three boards, and so on.

And, do not put pencils between the boards. Putting pencils at the edges creates space in the material being broken, and while a bunch of boards makes it look like karate breaking is awesome, the truth is that you can only break five or six boards with no spacers, but you can break up to 20 boards with spacers.

So be honest. Don't go for the yell of the crowd at a karate breaking demonstration...go for the inner satisfaction of being able to break only a piddling five or six boards with no spacers. This presents the question of whether you wish to impress impressionable young minds, or build your inner strength of character.

And, speaking of honest board breaking techniques, don't go leaving your boards out in the sun for a few days prior to your breaking exhibition. Dried boards break easier than regular boards. Like kindling, as a matter of fact.

But, on the same token, don't let your boards get wet before you break them. Your iron hand kung fu technique will turn into mushy hospital visitation rights.

And, that is about all there is to breaking boards, and, if you insist, upon karate breaking human skulls.

But...if you wish to do karate breaks on skulls, let me offer the obligatory caution: detached retinas, brain hemorrhage, fractured bones, and permanent neurological disorders. All of which translates to slurred and halting speech, let alone cauliflower ears and big, old puffy noses and...over 6 deaths a year in the boxing ring.

So practice your karate breaking technique, and do it for real, as if you really had to break a skull, but settle for perfection of character by resisting the urge to violence.

Here is an hilarious anecdote about a fellow who knocked himself out with karate breaking techniques. If you want to actually learn Karate well enough to break skulls, click on Matrix Karate at Monster Martial Arts.

How to Break Boards with Your Head Really Good!

Okay, we need a warning, like check with a doctor before you do this. Or maybe a psychiatrist. Or maybe just make sure you've backed up your brains on hard drive.

Back in 1968, I had just started Kenpo Karate, one of the Ed Parker offshoot branches, and the head instructor decided to put on a breaking seminar. I don't know what he was thinking, I don't think he had a side business selling insurance. At any rate, the potential for mayhem was lurking.

We entered the dojo and stacks of pine boards were waiting for us. As a group we were taught the theory of focusing, of punching through, and so on, and we were all excited. Then we started breaking the boards, one at a time, as the head instructor watched.

One of the guys, a fellow named Jeff, asked if it was possible to break a board with your head. The answer was yes, but it shouldn't be attempted until one was well trained. We then went into another room to break boards, and none noticed that Jeff wasn't with us.

We were in group discussion, and suddenly there was a tremendous thocking sound. It was such a unique sound that we all stopped what we were doing and stared at the door to the other room. The other room, where the sound came from, where Jeff had remained behind.

Suddenly, Jeff appeared at the door, he was standing aslant, and the look in his eyes was like little birdies singing. We all held our breaths as Jeff crossed the room, walking aslant, the birdies circling his head in a neat, little circling pattern. Jeff settled, well, sort of plonked, into a zen seated position, and the head instructor, with an eye on Jeff, continued his speechifying.

Now, if you're going to break a board with your head, and I don't care if you study Goju or Kyokushinkai or Hung Gar or whatever, work up to it. Start with thin boards, even an eighth of an inch, through a quarter, through 3/8s, and so on. Heck, even wear a football helmet the first few times, the potential for injury is that great.

Oh, and at the end of that seminar that I was at? Jeff came up to the head instructor after it was all over and asked, is it possible to break a board with your head. Maybe he should have worked on having the hardest punch instead of just a hard head!

Kenpo Karate Board Breaking with Head...Yikes!

I was studying Kenpo Karate back in 1967. I lived for Kumite (karate freestyle), and I thought that breaking was a subsection of martial arts reserved for the truly great.

I was excited, then, when I heard that a special board breaking seminar was going to be put on at my school.

On the appointed day we lined up and bowed in. There were about twenty of us, and we stared at the huge pile of boards that were waiting for our hardened fists and excited souls.

The head instructor, a slight fellow name of Rod, came to the head of the class and began telling us the things we needed to know. We learned the theory of how to tighten the fist, how to strike through the board, and how to have total and utter confidence!

One of the fellows, Jeff, raised his hand.

"Sir? Rod? Can you break a board with your head?"

Rod smiled, "Yes, but you need to practice hard, make sure you understand all the things you need to before you try such a thing."

Shortly afterwards we adjourned to another room to continue the seminar.

Jeff, however, was not with us.

Rod was going over how you have to hold the board, how you have to protect your fingers and brace the arms, when, suddenly, there was a sharp and loud THONK! from the other room.

Nobody said anything, we just held our breath and waited, and, suddenly, Jeff appeared at the doorway.

He was standing slanted. He walked off kilter across the room and knelt at the end of the line. Even his zazen was off kilter.

He was giving his total attention to Rod, however, so the seminar went on.

We broke a lot of boards that day, made a lot of kindling for winter, and at the end, everybody bowing to Rod and talking excitedly, Jeff made his way to the front of the class.

"Sir? Rod? Can you break a board with your head?"

He had no idea that he had ever asked that question before.

Are you a Kenpo martial artist? Check out The Man Who Killed Kenpo.

The Best But Cheapest Training Aid for Powerful Kicks

If you're like me, then you want powerful kicks that can knock a donkey on its tail. Sure, high Taekwondo kicks are good, but I want to lift that attacker's body up and send it sailing. Period.

I've looked at a ton of training aids over the years, and some work, some don't, some are expensive, but none of them has worked as well as the good old basic training aid you can pick up for a buck or two down at the orchard supply store. The training aid is fairly compact, and can be replaced quickly and easily should it break. The training aid I am speaking of is the basic eight by eight by sixteen cinder block.

First exercise is to simply kick over it. The reason you do this is to get a higher knee, which will allow you to drive a straighter line into your opponent's gut. You can easily stack blocks for different heights, and you can place them so you have to kick over them to hit a kicking bag.

Second exercise is to stand on the cinderblock and do your kicks. This is going to build balance, and strength in the balancing leg. It is fun to practice kicking in the four directions, and trains you to pivot quickly and easily.

Third exercise, you can put out four blocks and start doing your forms on them. You can go around and around, reverse direction, hop on and off, and your legs are going to get stronger and stronger and major stronger. Obviously, you're not going to have just powerful kicks, your stances and other movements are also going to get stronger.

Here are a couple of things you should know about training on cinder blocks. Make sure you learn how to lift your legs up and search for a landing place, should the block fall over. Also, start with them on side, practice a while, then stand them on end.

A cinder block weighs 29 pounds. That means you can take a couple of them, one in each arm, and do a little weight lifting. You can also, should you feel the urge, test your technique by smashing them with a foot or fist.

In closing, cinder blocks are the cheapest training aid, and they can be replaced and used in various ways. Also, there are a bunch of different things you can do, which things are all basic and relate directly to strength and agility. Guaranteed, use these cheapies for a while and you will have mucho powerful kicks!

Best Martial Arts Equipment for the Money!

You guys may think that this is a tongue in check article on getting the best martial arts equipment, but it isn't. I have personally tried the methods here, and they are top notch body calisthenic methods.

First, I tried cinderblocks. I didn't want to dig holes and sink poles for the Plum Flower Fist, which is a form of Praying Mantis Gung Fu. This was great. Jumping up down gave me strength, as well improving my balance.

From there I look for other things to use for martial arts equipment.

Tires were great. I learned to use tires originally for swinging a wooden sword. Took a lot of strength and control to make the tire turn and bounce the way you wanted it to. So I grabbed nine of them, arranged them in a simple grid of three by three, and started walking the circle, Pa Kua Chang style. This was odd, hard to ground through the springiness of the tires. but, you often learn more from what doesnt' work than what does, so I moved on.

My my next experiment in Martial Arts Training Equipment. I put four by fours on edge and practiced forms on them. This was interesting, and taken directly from Ton Toi Northern Shaolin Gung Fu. Ton Toi means springy legs, and I learned all sorts of things about balance while springing from beam to beam.

And, I tried doing forms on top of fences. It was wild. Trying to spin and move, six feet above the ground, without falling al-l-l the way down! I don't know how much I got out of this martial arts equipment, but if was fun!

And, in between these things I tried hanging balls from the rafters, punching tennis balls at a wall, and other sorts of things. But my next big foray into martial arts equipment was at the old Los Angeles Zoo.

The old zoo, now sort of gone, or at least redone into a picnic area, was a mess of cages and bounders strewn about in the cages to give the animals some sort of sense of nature. So I worked out in cages...lions and tiger and me...oh my!

And I learned a lot! I especially grew in arm strength. Having to hang on to the side of a cage, or going across the top monkey style, built up a lot of strength in the arms. Trying to do kicks while so perched was especially educated. You get a whole new appreciation for how the hip joints work.

Now, last in my martial arts equipment were trees. At the Los Angeles zoo there were all sorts of low hanging trees. I could walk on the trunks of some of them, climb to joints, and generally swing around and do all sorts of stuff. The interesting thing about this was that I could practice sinking my weight.

One of the places I got this idea from, aside from my experiences in the cages, was a fellow wrote an article where he had to hang from a tree limb for an hour a day for a few months before the master would teach him.

Well, having done a little hanging myself, I can definitely attest to the benefits in the arms and shoulders. It stretches them out and gives truth to the old saying, 'A long muscle is a strong muscle.'

Now, that about does it except for one thing...all of the equipment I used cost nothing. That's right, I didn't have to spend any money at my martial arts equipment suppliers, and I got a better work out than some big nautilus machine could ever give!

A Dynamic Kung Fu Wooden Dummy the Easy Way

The kung fu wooden dummy is a fantastic training device. It toughens the arms for blocking, it toughens the palms for striking, and it is an opponent that never quits, but always loses. Unfortunately, it costs a bit much, so here are a couple of alternatives to help the wooden dummy aficionado.

The Kung Fu Wooden Dummy is popular in many martial arts, but the main art is Wing Chun Ving Tsun) Gung Fu. This art has practiced with the wooden man for the longest, and even has a complete form for dominating it. Other arts, however, use the dummy, also.

This writer recalls seeing the Kung Fu wooden dummy in Jackie Chan's Rumble in the Bronx. Seeing the dust fly when Jackie lays into it is a wondrous moment. Possibly the best chop sockie to feature the wooden figure is Ip Man, with Donny Yen.

In the beginning the martial artist will become adept at pounding on kicking bags and speed bags, and perhaps toughening the fists on the makiwara. It won't be long, however, until the karateka or kung fu practitioner puts a couple of rug samples on a tree and moves into tougher fist conditioning. The trick, however, is to get the arm to fly out at you so you can block it.

This writer made a simple striking tool by wrapping a towel around a pole, and then having people jab at him with it. This rapidly turned into an advanced form of freestyle, where the block had to be done, and the distance to the pole holder closed. It is quite challenging to dash three or four feet in a moment to negate the distance the pole offers.

From there one might consider mounting a pole on a pivot. Simply bury a two by four in the earth, then place a moveable pole atop it. On can block the pole, and block it again when it swings around, and even get into ducking and blocking.

Eventually, one will want to get a large piece of wood-a log-drill holes through it, and set up some arms and even legs. One can then dance back and forth, palm the wooden limbs, and pretend that one is fighting a real opponent. What is really nifty is to put some large springs on the limbs so that there is a certain amount of give and take.

The cost of wood being what it is, or perhaps the difficulty of procuring a log in a city, one might consider alternative materials. PVC might work, if one could find thick enough plastic that won't break, or perhaps even some sort of metal. This type of material would require towels or other material being wrapped around it to protect the arms and fists.

In closing, there are many ways to set up a fake opponent, and the martial artist is limited only by his imagination. Watch movies, read books, and start inspecting the materials available to you. Guaranteed, a kung fu wooden dummy will go a long way in your martial arts training.

KARATE

My Brother's Bloody Knuckles...and Real Karate

I remember the time my brother came home and his knuckles were all bloody.

Now, I looked up to my brother, and I quickly asked, "Did you get in a fight? Did you hit somebody?"

"Nah. I was just practicing Karate."

Practicing Karate? This was back in the sixties, and it was a new word for me. But it wasn't long before I found the book he had been reading.

Super Karate Made Easy, by Moja Rone.

Never found out who Moja was, but it didn't matter, he had done his damage.

You see, while it sold millions, and was one of the first big books, probably the first mass produced book, on Karate, it was lacking in...shall we say Common Sense?

And my brother had been out punching telephone poles until his knuckles were bloody because that was supposed to toughen them up, give him a fist that bad guys would be scared of!

But it really gave him a fist that doctors would be scared of, and laid serious groundwork for hands that wouldn't work, arthritis, and other maladies that go along with abusing the human body.

Years later I would enter my first Karate class, and I punched air.

That's right, I practiced on that great villain...air.

But my hands didn't get bloody and swell up and become unworkable, and I learned how to focus my awareness. To snap the fist. To tighten upon impact. And when I did eventually start hitting things, the tightness of the hand and the object I was hitting protected me.

And what was I hitting?

The human body.

That's right, we budding Karate students would do our techniques on each other, and that included striking the body.

And I learned how to go gentle, because I wanted others to go gentle on me.

And I learned to hit harder, because I wanted my technique to be effective.

And I learned what a body felt like, and the correct places to hit the body, and, somewhere in there, I stopped caring about hitting the human body.

Oh, a body is a great feedback device, but when I learned that I could hurt another human body...I didn't want my own body to be hurt.

Thus, real Karate is learning to be dangerous, learning how to fight back, but it is also learning how to be gentle.

Karate means empty hands, and that is hands without weapons, and, in the end, a hand that is not just a weapon, but it is also not a weapon.

The Best Karate Course in the World is actually available online. Just kick your mouse over to Kang Duk Won.

Take a Punch and Walk Away Smiling with One Simple Exercise

Take a punch is something every karate fighter has to do. Only a fool would assume that he could walk out of a karate match, or a kung fu fight or taekwondo contest, without taking a punch. So this article is going to tell you how to survive getting hit.

First, it goes without saying that you are going to need conditioning, and plenty of it. This is going to be very specific conditioning, but if you are in good condition then you will know if you can take a punch. This conditioning will cover the torso and the head, as they are the primary targets in a fight.

You should concentrate on the basic body calisthenics such as sit ups, push ups, and that sort of thing. Honestly, you should be able to do hundreds of them, and with no effort. If you can do them with no effort, your body is going to be tight and taut and able to absorb punches with ease.

The head is a different matter, as there aren't any easy exercises to 'strengthen' the head. But one can survive a strike to the head if they understand what actually happens to the head when it gets hit. Understanding the 'impact process' will enable you to take punches with just one simple exercise.

When the head gets hit the brain bounces around inside the skull. The trick, then, is to position the head so that it doesn't move much. The way to do this is to strengthen the neck muscles.

The way to strengthen the neck muscles, the one simple exercise, is to hold a tennis ball under the chin while training. This not only strengthens the neck, but it positions the head forward, which is good for bobbing and weaving and ducking under. Furthermore, when one does get hit the force goes down the neck, instead of creating a 'whiplash effect' in the head.

Now, when one is doing Karate or kung fu, one should be fighting more from a distance, using the legs, and keeping the head out of the action. However, as the fight closes, as the distance collapses, one should intuitively lower the head, make it more 'bull like.' This will enable one to slip the punches, and to even deflect them to the shoulders.

In closing, do a lot of basic body conditioning, old standards like sit ups, crunches, push ups, dips, pull ups, and that sort of thing. Specifically for the head, do the tennis ball under the chin trick to strengthen the neck. Whether it is the ring, a street fight, or even a karate match or kung fu contest, it's not a pleasant thing to get hit, but with a little work you will be able to take a punch and walk away smiling.

A Real Reason for the Development of Classical Karate!

The very first move of Karate, as taken from the first Heian or Pinan form, is a step to the side with a low block. But Karate was not designed for blocking. Yes, there are blocks in the art, and it can be adapted to blocking and striking modes, but it was not designed for blocking except by the way.

Karate was designed for imperial bodyguards to guard the king of Okinawa. These bodyguards were supposed to use their art in a room filled with warriors from different countries. Warriors who would have different weapons and ways of fighting, while the Okinawans had to remain unarmed.

Thus, would you block a samurai sword? Would you try to deflect a bullet? Because these were the real weapons that the bodyguards had to face.

Consider also that the first command a general might give his troops, if they were to attempt to kidnap the king of Okinawa, would be to restrain the bodyguards. This means that samurai would step forward and grab arms, perhaps preparatory to tying the hands of the bodyguards, or merely herding them from the room, or otherwise controlling them. And this means that the first defense of the bodyguards, as described by the first technique in the first form, would be to step in, dropping the weight and arm, thus escaping from the technique, and possibly head butting those who tried to grab them.

That's right, an escape from a grab, then a violent step forward to close with and punch and shove the samurai, or whoever the warriors were. This would cause chaos and confusion. This would allow the king to escape.

Now, examine the form, look at it. This is the only way it makes sense. This is the start of what the bodyguards who created the art had in mind.

If the samurai drew a sword, the bodyguard had to rush the samurai. This is the reason for the big steps in the form, to enable the bodyguards to get close enough to maim and destroy. This explains the moves of forms that, otherwise, don't make sense.

If a samurai attempted to grab, charge into them, head butting, then push them. This is the secret of the first technique, and this is how the art was designed to work. Thinking about the techniques in this way reveals an art that is true beyond belief, but you are going to have to put aside the way you were taught, and take further steps down this path if you are going to find the true art of karate.

Creating The Perfect Body With Shotokan, Uechi Ryu, Or Another Karate System!

You want to have a perfectly designed body, and Isshin Ryu, Goju Ryu, or some other Karate System is the key! There are, however, several things you should understand before you begin this journey. These things would be what, exactly, a perfect body is.

To be honest, a perfect body is going to have to do with proportion. One of the best definitions of proportions I have come across is by Leo DaVinci. His analysis of frame is as follows: length the same as height, seven heads high, three heads shoulder to shoulder, two heads from fingers to elbows, four heads hips to toes, and so on.

Now, DaVinci is said to have changed these measurements to fit his sculpting designs. I don't know if he really did, I am just curious concerning the correct idea of proportion. I am interested as to whether doing the Martial Arts will grow shape of the body until it resembles these measurements.

The second thing to estimate is what type of martial arts you should study. Here we must change the direction of our analysis, and look at the two types of schools in original Karate studies. These would be the shorei and shorin karate styles.

One of the schools trains one to be light and nimble, and is probably for a light and nimble body. The other school trains one to hold their ground, and would indicate a more sold and bulky body that is not so agile. Obviously, you should design your art, and the karate forms you study, and the karate bunkai that you do, to fit one or the other of these schools.

Thus far we have analyzed the measurements of the perfect karate body, and we have discussed the two methods of training in traditional karate.

Next we need to consider the workings of the ideal structure. This would depend, of course, on which types of katas you have decided to train in.

Many people want the large, muscular body, and they wouldn't necessarily be correct. Size and mass, you see, is something you have to lug around. It would be better for your overall ability to move to have leaner, more dense muscles.

Thus, you should design your muscles so they have enough mass or speed to create impact, but not so large that they tire out. To be exact, it's nice to think about being the terminator, but the reality of combat should gear you towards a lean, mean body that is quick, agile, and will last all day long. This should be one of the most important considerations when you think about utilizing Isshin Ryu, Goju Ryu or any other Karate System to create the perfect Body.

To have a Perfect Karate Body you need a Perfect 'Style' of Karate. Head on over over to LearnKarateOnline.net to find that perfection.

Japanese Martial Arts Replaced by One Punch Karate Mistake!

A student recently asked me why Karate became popular in Japan, when the Japanese had their own Martial Arts. The answer to this question is in an historical incident. And, the answer reveals something rather sordid about the human nature.

If you've ever watched a Chinese Kung Fu movie, the plot will invariably turn to the infamous western boxing match. The boxing match did occur about 1900, though the results were invariably not as the movies would have you believe. Indeed, the whole incident actually exploits the common mans need for myth and legend, and a way to bolster up a sagging belief in oneself.

That said, one of these infamous boxing matches occurred in Japan in 1921. An Okinawan by the name of Choki Motobu was in Japan. He was descended from a royal family, was a brawler in his youth, but had studied much Karate.

Motobu was not too successful at business, accounts have it that he was out of work and broke. A friend convinced him to enter a Western Boxing contest which had offered to 'take on all comers.' Motobu was 52 at the time.

Accounts of the match vary. Some have Motobu evading the taller western boxer for several rounds, then pouncing in and knocking out the Russian strong man with one punch. Other accounts claim Motobu kicked his man in the groin, and when the fellow bent over in agony, struck him with a foul blow.

Whatever the truth, Motobu was the winner, and the crowd went wild. The press, anxious to report on this upset and vindication of race, searched frantically for an image to run with the story. They came up with an old file image of...Gichin Funakoshi.

Thus, the story of why Japan became enthralled with Karate may have more to do with dirty fighting, lazy reporting, and a people in search of a superior identity, than with any superiority of art. That said, however, this writer makes no indictment of Karate, nor does he hold any martial art as superior. That is not the point to be made here.

This is merely a history lesson, and a revelation concerning mans poor self image of himself, and how that image can be exploited. When you hear somebody claim that one art is better than another, one should consider the tale of Motobu Choki and why Japan chose Karate as a 'national art.' And that is how Japanese Martial Arts were supplanted by a One Punch Karate Mistake.

Gichin Funakoshi and the True History of Karate!

The Common misconception is that Gichin Funakoshi is the father of modern Karate. Well, he could be considered such, except that something odd happened a century ago, that puts a blot on this conception. We've got to give him credit for spreading the art, but was it the true art?

I know what I write here is not going to be the most popular article I ever wrote, there will be a few people who are going to want to take me to task. However, the history that I am about to tell you really happened, it is the truth. That said, please know that I do respect Gichin Funakoshi and what he did for Karate.

In turn of the century, last century, Japan, people, same as people all over, loved the human cockfight. It wasn't uncommon for people to gather to watch gladiatorial contests between different arts and artists. Certain of these gladiators even offered open challenges to the audience, step up if you think you can beat me.

One night a Russian strongman issued a challenge to the Japanese audience. One can imagine the sneering challenge, and the surprise when a frumpy, old Okinawan stepped up to the ring and prepared to fight. The year was 1921, and the turning point for karate was about to occur.

Motobu Chōki was 52 years old when he stepped into the ring that night. He had studied with virtually every Okinawan Karate master in Okinawa, and he had, when he was young and impetuous, honed his art in the violent red light districts of his island home. This history, and a daily regimen of makiwara, and perhaps the hint of royal blood and pride in his veins, served him in good stead.

One punch later, a punch almost too fast to be seen, Motobu climbed out of the ring, the Russian strongman lay sprawled and snoozing the fist snooze. Reporters went wild, wrote their stories, and submitted them to the editors. Editors went wild, and, since they didn't have any photos of Motobu, but they did have a picture of a guy doing karate, they popped in the wrong picture.

So Gichin Funakoshi, a mild school teacher from Okinawa, got credit for the violent knock out and ultimate karate prowess of Motobu Choki. And Motobu, though he did teach karate and have an effect, because he wasn't fluent in the japanese language, and because the media did such a bang up job of reporting, got no credit. And Funakoshi is credited with spreading Karate to the world, yet, it wouldn't have happened without Motobu's one punch one kill competence and attitude.

Now, who has the real karate, a school teacher who shmoozed with the Japanese because of the wrong picture and good communication skills, or a rough cob who got the job done. No, Funakoshi's karate is not bad, and generations of karateka have worked to improve it. However, there is still that one blot, a hundred years ago, provided by a man with a slobber knocker punch, which offers the concept of who had the True Art.

The Facts of Shotokan Karate

Shotokan was developed by Master Gichin Funakoshi, a school teacher from Okinawa, and his son, Gigo Funakoshi.   Master Funakoshi trained in the the two major Okinawan styles of Nahate, Shorei-ryu and Shorin-ryu. Shotokan is a combination of the two. His style is true to the changes made in Nahate by Anko Itosu (the introduction of hte Heian forms). He did change the names of the kata to make them easier for the Japanese to pronounce. He never named his Karate, merely referred to it as Karate.

The first splash in the Shotokan saga came as a result of a match held in Japan in the 1920s. A fellow name of Choki Motobu attended a match, accepted the challenge by the westerner to 'defeat all comers,' and knocked out the 'champ.'

The press, unfortunately, had no pictures of Mr. Motobu, so they substituted one of Gichin Funakoshi. As a result, Mr. Motobu went home, and Gichin Funakoshi put on a series of demonstrations which established his art as the predominant Karate in Japan.

Shotokan received a severe boost in popularity with the inclusion of that art in the curriculum of the universities. Young students studied the art, and were exported to the world to share the art.

In 1957 Master Funakoshi died, and with him died the cohesiveness of the Shotokan organization. While the major split was between the Japan Karate Association (headed by Masatoshi Nakayama) and the Shotokai (Motonobu Hironishi and Shigeru Egami) other groups also made their appearance. Thus, there is not a single 'Shotokan school,' and all schools bear the mark of Master Funakoshi.

The name Shotokan is actually the name of the first training hall (dojo) that Master Funakoshi built. This was in 1939 at Mejiro. It was destroyed in 1945 during an allied bombing.

The word Shotokan means 'pine waves,' which represents the movement of pine needles when the wind blows through them.

Shoto was Funakoshi's pen name, and Kan means House. Thus, Shotokan means 'Funakoshi's house.

Shotokan is considered a 'hard style' martial art. It is taught in three main parts: Kihon (basics), Kata (forms), and Kumite (freestyle fighting). It teaches the student to take long, low stances, and to generate immense amounts of power. As students progress they learn more fluid movements, and even throws such as one would find in martial arts such as Aikido.

The philosophy of Shotokan was laid out by Gichin Funakoshi in the Twenty Precepts of Karate. These precepts are based on bushido and zen principles.

The main principles known by most students, however, are the five rules for training in the dojo.
Seek perfection of character
Be faithful
Endeavor to excel
Respect others
Refrain from violent behavior.

The 'golden rule' of Shotokan, however, is: "The ultimate aim of Karate lies not in victory or defeat, but in the perfection of the character of the participant."

The practice of Kata is the major training method in Shotokan, and these patterns were laid out by Master Funakoshi in his writings. Chief of these writings is 'Karate-Do: The Master Text.' Following are the 26 (of 27 recommended by Funakoshi)) Kata practiced by many schools.

Heian shodan

Heian nidan

Heian sandan

Heian yondan

Heian godan

Bassai dai

Jion

Empi

Kanku dai

Hangetsu

Jitte

Gankaku

Tekki shodan

Tekki nidan

Tekki sandan

Nijūshiho

Chinte

Sōchin

Meikyō

Unsu

Bassai shō

Kankū shō

Wankan

Gojūshiho shō

Gojūshiho dai

Ji'in

Karate, Dark Alleys, and Gloopy Aliens!

Good Morning USA, and world, and, uh, guess I'll throw in the universe. Never can tell, some gloopy alien with three eyes might be keeping track of those strange critters on earth. Might be reading this article right now making sure we're not being contentious and guilty of sedition to the alien galactic empire.

Hi, Gloopy Alien. Wonder if he knows what this here finger is for? Heh.

Speaking of Gloopy Aliens, Gichin Funakoshi, the founder of modern Karate, was about 80 years old, and was out for a walk. The night was gloomy, Japan was in a state of unrest, and he saw a thug lurking on the street corner. And he knew, just knew, that that thug was going to try to mug him.

Hey, you think a mugger's going to pick on somebody big? Nah, muggers want to do their work with the least amount of risk, you know? Smart guys, these muggers.

Anyway, Gichin keeps on walking makes sure he looks feeble, and as he passes the mugger and the mugger leaps at him he whirls and grabs the mugger. Now, you might be wondering where he grabbed the mugger. A death lock on the carotid--a specialized nerve center that immobilizes totally?

Well, uh, no. He grabbed him by the, um, chestnuts. The cajones, you know..the apples.

He grabbed him by his future, his children to be, his only reason for fun on those long, lonely nights that besiege a mugger when he is all alone and can't find a date. Now the founder of Karate has a mugger by the embarrassment what is his next technique? Does he execute a half fist to the throat and pop the Adam's apple...or at least shove it down the unworthy's own throat?

Does he execute a spearhand to the chest and pluck the mugger's heart out and take a bite while the horrified mugger watches in horror? Or does he just...squeeze. Slowly, squeeze, and watch the blood drain out of the mugger's face, and the life out of his body, and the joy out of his future?

Squeeze...so that the nutty pulp runs out from between his gnarly, old fingers. Squeeze...until a loud popping sound fills the night air. Squeeze, until the mugger screams like a little girl and falls to the pavement, never to enjoy the feel of loving again.

Gichin called for the cops. Yep, he stood on that corner and held that man and called for help. And the mugger was totted away to think about his crimes, and the terror of having his manhood held by another man.

An interesting lesson for a mugger, eh? Another interesting lesson would be if you looked up the real meaning of the word testament and where it comes from and all that. Anyway, the point of all this is this...don't walk down that dark alley.

Yep. My students have heard me say this, and they know what I mean. When you have a choice of a long walk down a lit street, or a short trip through a dark alley, take the long way.

You can tell you've made it, that you do understand what the martial arts are all about when you can see a dark alley before you reach it. Hey, a sunny street in the heart of town might be a dark alley if there's some idiot waiting for you. And you should have developed the extra perception, through those endless hours of practice, to know the difference between a dark alley and a well lit street.

Funakoshi says Karate is not the Karate It Was!

The only thing that stays the same is that everything changes. That is the truth of this universe. That this is true in Karate (and other martial arts) is shown in the words of Gichin Funakoshi, the father of Modern Karate.

Before I tell you his words, let me make a point through the words of Matsu Basho. Follow not in the footsteps of the masters, but rather seek what they sought. While this article may seem like an attack on traditionalism, it is really merely an admonishment to look deep.

To look deep is to find the soul. To look deep is to find the true martial arts. To look deep is to find yourself.

Hoping to see Karate included in the universal physical education taught in our public schools, I set about revising the kata so as to make them as simple as possible. Times change, the world changes, and obviously the martial arts must change too. The Karate that high school students practice today is not the same Karate that was practiced even as recently as ten years ago [this book was written in 1956], and it is a long way indeed from the Karate I learned when I was a child in Okinawa.

The preceding paragraph are the words of Gichin Funakoshi. There may be some paraphrasing or substitution of terms, so if you want the real quote, simply look in his book. Karate-Do: My Way of Life.

The point here is that to memorize what has gone before is fine, up to a point. And at that point one must give up the Monkey See Monkey Do instruction and start digging. This is the only way to truly learn the real martial arts.

The Martial Arts, and we are speaking specifically of Karate here, were created for specific times to solve exact problems. Was it designed for defense against weapons that are no longer in use, armor that is no longer worn, mind sets that are no longer showing? Was it translated for children, for different cultures, for languages and beliefs and mind sets?

The answer is yes, Karate has changed over the years, and not always for the best. Thus, one must look beyond technique, beneath words, and beyond even the visions of our teachers. One must look deeply and long, else one will never realize that Karate is not what it was, and they will miss the sight of oneself.

The Truth About the Failure of Classical Karate!

Karate, as it is done in modern times, is absolutely nothing like the Karate invented centuries ago. There are many reasons for this, cultural, historical, vested interest, and on and on. This article will pin point the exact reasons Karate has changed, and it is considered a failure in the eyes of many people.

Karate was developed to defend the king of Okinawa. The techniques gathered together were specific in their intent, and that intent was shaped by having to deal with a variety of soldiers and weaponry. Interestingly, Karate had very little to do with blocking and striking, though that can be considered as valid, and more to do with disarming and maiming.

The Japanese eventually commanded the King of Okinawa to come live in Japan, where he was treated like a guest, but still in prison. With the king gone, what reason did the bodyguards have to study their art? Thus, lessons were taught to children to make them strong, but the maiming and butchery of the pure art was left out.

Eventually, Karate was brought to Japan, where it proved not only adequate, but more than comparable to the arts of the Japanese. One must remember, however, that the Japanese had stolen the king of the Okinawans. Thus, it is doubted whether, if the teachers even knew the true art at this point, whether they would teach the people who had stolen their king.

The next step in the evolution of Karate came when the Americans conquered Japan. They did this by dropping an atomic bomb, and now we have the same scene as described in the last paragraph. One has to ask whether the Japanese, if they even knew the true art, would teach the people who had dropped an atomic bomb on them.

Now the art reaches America. It is commercialized, dumbed down for children, and geared around tournaments. People are more concerned about belts and the latest fight night than they are about the knowledge potential of the art.

Finally, the art starts to fail. People refer to MacDojo's in disgust, and the brutality of MMA, at least workable, is held up to the light. Yet, I ask the question...what was the original art?

What is that art that was designed to maim and destroy in defense of honor and king? What is that art that plumbs the soul and reveals the depths of the man? I say it is still there, the true martial art is still there...you just have to be willing to look for it and work for it.

What Happened to Mess Up Karate!

Back in the fifties Karate hit the United States. Advertisements showed men killing bulls, and promised that a slight woman could beat up a grown man. Why, even a child. using this wonderful science called Karate, could accomplish amazing feats.

So what happened? What happened is that there was such demand for the art that there weren't enough teachers. And we must now ask ourselves what, exactly, does a person need to teach Karate?

Back then, guys with three years experience were getting their black belts, and then turning around and teaching. But it took a dozen years to master the art back then, and an instructor needs more data than a master. Being a master means that you have the data, but being a teacher means that you not only have the data, but you can get somebody else to get it.

Fast forward a few decades. You've got guys teaching the martial arts, and they have twenty years experience, and they've mastered the art, but nobody ever taught them how to teach. Experience will make a master, not too much trouble, but simple experience will not make an instructor.

So the instructor needs actual data. He doesn't just need more extreme classes on how to beat people up, he needs to find out the reasons why things work, and be able to impart those reason to other people. The real problem, you see, is one of education.

So you want to take karate, and you walk into a school and observe a teacher. Is the teacher explaining why things work? Or is he merely asking people to mimic him?

Yes, Monkey see monkey do is the first stage, but it only lasts a few minutes. The real information of why something works must be inserted, or what is being taught will become an exercise of memorization. And when the mugger comes at you, do you want to remember how to defend yourself, or do you want to have the instantaneous intuition that is available if you don't just memorize, but know and understand the how and the why of why the moves are what they are?

So there is it. A martial art that could do all it claimed, but was savaged by quick black belts who wanted to make money, and who didn't take the time to ask why they were doing what they were doing. I trust this information will help you when you seek an instructor, and when you are undergoing instruction.

KANG DUK WON

Are Old Time Martial Arts Better?

You always hear the term about 'the good, old days.' And, in the martial arts, this is really true. I always hear people thinking back to when men were men, and sheep were...you know.

But it is a legitimate question.

On one hand, you have the great arts coming out of the orient. I was studying back in the sixties and seventies, so the main arts were judo and karate, with a smattering of Kung Fu. We studied in in dirty dojos and did manic drills. We brooked no nonsense, and we were patient with beginners.

On the other hand, you have designer water, contracts and classes in the Y, at the gym, down on the corner, and in every friend's garage.

So, my personal opinion is that the martial arts were better. I started at a McDojo, then went to a classical Korean Karate school (Kang Duk Won).

The McDojo was the state of art to come, with thick mats and air conditioning and tournament freestyle and contracts and good looking chickies.

The Kang Duk Won had a mat that had been ripped and stitched so many times it was like walking across Frankenstein's face. The bag went to the cobbler's every week. We packed our own bags for better texture and weight and resistance to our endless kicks. Warn't no chickies allowed.

The McDojo had shiny trophies, high fives for points, and you pressed your gi before class.

The Kang Duk Won you did hundreds of kicks, you didn't wash your gi, and you couldn't press the clutch down because your shins were so badly bruised.

In modern times we have scientific achievements that enable one to get more strength in the muscle.

Of course, modern times has a lot of junk science and internet gimmicks, so...?

Now, it's pretty obvious which way I am biased. I was there, I don't think Alzheimer's has obscured my memories of those old work outs, and I have seen modern schools that teach 18 arts on their front sign, but are a jumble of bags and exercise equipment inside.

But, nobody made me God, and if you think otherwise, then go ahead and tear me a new one. Heck, I might even learn something!

And, if you are old school like me, then feel free to leave your memory. Heck, it might just become legend!

Your Martial Art Doesn't Work the Hells Angel Said

I had studied Chinese Kenpo Karate for two years. I was an instructor, and I had written the training manual for my school.Then I ran into a Hells's Angel.

The story actually started when the restaurant I was working at hired a geeky looking kid. I didn't like him much, but then one day I saw him kick a wall. The wall shook like the 1906 earthquake, and I knew that he knew something I didn't.

So I got to know him, and he said he studied Kang Duk Won Korean Karate. He said he didn't know it well, which I found hard to believe because I had seen him kick a wall harder than a donkey kicks a pervert. He said, however, that his brother knew a lot more than him, and let's go talk to him.

So that night, I think it was a Tuesday, we went down to a house in Sunnyvale to meet his brother. As we pulled up Alex said to me, "I should probably tell you that my brother is a Hells Angel." I blinked, but, naive me, heck...I knew Kenpo, right?

His brother was maybe five foot ten, a little shorter than me, but he had the outlaw look in his eyes. We talked for a while, and then he simply said, "Your Martial Art doesn't work." Then he grabbed me by the shirt front with two of the gnarliest fists I had ever seen and told me to work my first technique on him, and then he named the technique.

I went into action. I locked his fists with one hand and brought my other hand up to break his elbows, I struck his wrists with my radial paralyzing downward chop, and when I went to chop him in the throat he threw me through a wall. Yep, all the way through a wall.

He laughed and helped me up, and then he told me to grab his shirt front. I did, and he showed me the self defense technique from his martial arts school. He reached over and punched me in the chest so hard that...that's right, I went right through the wall again.

Now, this is a true story, and this experience changed my life, definitely changed the way I was studying martial arts, and prompted me down the road to other martial arts and how to really make them work. I spent seven years at the Kang Duk Won, worked alongside all manner of people, including hells angels and other outlaw bikers. And I definitely learned why a martial art doesn't work.

The Difference Between Kang Duk Won and classical Karate

It's sort of funny to say classical Karate, because Kang Duk Won actually came before traditional Karate. The classical approach came about during the forties and fifties in Japan. Kang Duk Won came from a line before that, from a classmate of Gichin Funakoshi.

Now, there are quite a few differences between classical Karate and the Kang Duk Won, and I could go through the various stances and point to various things having to do with body alignment and the correct way to achieve it. But that is included in 'The Master Instructor Course,' and I would rather point to a single instance that may be more significant.

In my forties I was practicing punching, and I discovered, one day, that when I did a full power punch I was getting a headache.

But I don't get headaches! Hadn't gotten headaches for years! So I began examining what I was doing.

When I was punching I was using so much force that I was actually giving myself whiplash. Simply, the force of the punch, the shoulders and neck being jerked, I was getting whiplash and a headache.

Hmm. Something wrong there. But that was the way I had been punching for decades!

Well, my body was getting older.

I could make it stronger with calisthenics, perhaps reduce and defeat the headache phenomena, but...I didn't want to do calisthenics! I wanted to do Karate!

So I changed the way I was doing things. I simply started punching less hard, and focusing more snap into the wrist, and I found out something interesting: less effort was giving me more power!

Now that was odd, to say the least! How could punching easier make for harder punches?

Then I thought about various Kung Fu things I had read. And then I thought about my instructor, who had been whiplike and effortless. I thought about how I had not been the fastest student, had had to struggle for what others were getting...effortlessly.

My instructor once told me: 'A tight fist is a heavy fist.' But I hadn't understood it! He actually meant that I should tighten only my fist! Not my whole body!

So I began doing Karate keeping my body loose, not tightening the whole thing upon impact, but only snapping the fist.

I learned how to keep the tan tien taut so it could take a punch, but not to make the belly tight. And I found that this type of tautness enabled me to send chi out into the rest of my body more efficiently.

I learned that tightening the body, or the body parts, locks the energy and reduces motion...and the circulation of chi.

And, I learned how to snap so efficiently that I could put out a candle from over a foot away. I detail that, and show the video, in 'The Punch.'

Isn't it funny how we listen, but don't learn? Fortunately, if we keep practicing, the words will eventually make sense.

At any rate, if you look at classical Karate there is an obsession with power. In the Kang Duk Won there is an obsession with...loose form. Yes, we tighten, but only the tool, and not the whole body.

It is much more efficient, enables you to do longer work outs, enables you to channel chi better, and all sorts of other things.

And that is the difference, at least on one simple level, between classical Karate and the Kang Duk Won.

What is the Slant of the Kang Duk Won

Every Martial Art is slanted, and the Kang Duk Won is no different.

Sometimes the slant of the martial art can be bad, sometimes good. In the case of the Kang Duk Won...

the slant is very, very good.

The first real influence on Kang Duk Won was probably Joon Byung In. Before then the art wGunas pure Karate, straight out of Okinawa, as taught by Kanken Toyama. Toyama probably offered a direct transmission from the Okinawan Imperial bodyguards, who invented the art.

Yes, one could say that Karate is a slant on earlier martial arts, specifically Chinese Kung Fu, but then we are really talking about the alteration of systems, and not just a slant.

Joon Byung In had trained in a Chinese Martial Art previously, so one would think that there would be a Kung Fu slant to it. If there is, I think it would be in the training drills, perhaps the seven step punching exercise.

But I don't think the slant on the forms would be much.

Remember that Joon's Kang Duk Won was at the heart of many of the Kwans in Korea at the time, and the gross movements of the forms are fairly much the same.

The second potential for slant would be by Bob Babich. Mr. Babich was short and thin, and he tended to make the art a very straight line affair. He turned his rear foot in in the back stance almost like a sprinter, and this speaks of a very straight line intention.

The thing here is that Bob was a black Belt instructor in Kyokushinkai before he came into the Kang Duk Won. Yet when I examine the forms I see no hint of Kyokushinkai. So it seems as if Mr. Babich left the Kyokushinkai complete, and thus there would be virtually no slant from that quarter.

In the end, using matrixing and having over 40 years to inspect the thing, I didn't find much slant, and only a spattering of influence.

Byung In Joon seems to have put aside his earlier training in favor of the Kang Duk Won, as does Robert Babich.

This speaks highly of the system, that it would remain pure no matter who touched it. When one does the system they feel the spiritual essence, and they realize that this is more than fighting, it is survival. And, as one travels through the system one comes in contact with a unique awareness that gives one an elevated outlook upon life, and changes the way one interacts with his fellow man and the universe itself.

The Seven Things My Karate Instructor Told Me

I studied Karate for some seven years, and in that time my Karate instructor told me seven things.

I should say first that he didn't tell me anything else.

He was a silent man, and he would sit in his office, students clustered around, and the students did all the talking. He would give a yes or no, but even a lot of that. He would just smile and enjoy.

Big difference from most people, who really don't know when to shut up.

And, the odd thing I noticed, the more people talk the less they say; they are like radios set to some station of static and left to chatter.

'There are many roads to the top of the mountain.' He told me that one when I asked him which art was best.

'A tight fist is a heavy fist.' He was admonishing me to understand the 'loose-tight' concept of the fist. We of the Kang Duk Won, you see, were not encouraged to make our whole bodies rigid. The better a student was, the less tight his body was, and the more tight his fist, and only his fist, was. Surrounding that fist was silence. Emptiness. A dearth of chatter. No talk.

'How's work?' He used to ask everybody that when they entered the school. It was his way to get us to start the conversation.

Once I asked him what the difference between 'The Way,' and a method was. He asked me if there was one, and he did it in a way to let me know that there wasn't one. How interesting. It was the death of mysticism for me, or at least let me know that he wasn't bent on the mystical approach.

'I just do the forms. Everything is in the forms.' I had asked him how he got so good, and it was part of a larger question about what he studied, how did he keep learning now that he was at the top.

'Want a drink?' A real ice breaker if there ever was one. But it was an ice breaker for us, not him. He was already totally and truly comfortable with himself; he lived, and he knew it, and he loved it.

'Wham!' Yes, he would actually say 'Wham! when he was emphasizing a point. He would set up the technique, glancing at you to make sure you were paying attention, and then he would do the technique, liquid lightening, and say 'Wham!' instead of kia-ing.

That's it.

When he taught a form he did so almost completely silently. He just showed, repeating as needed, in small sections for the white belts, and almost whole forms, and only once or twice, when we were black belts.

Past that, he instructed by example, by doing intently and with more focus than any human being I've ever seen.

Here's the thing, people who talk haven't done the forms enough, haven't sunk their awareness into the forms deeply enough to become the forms, and to have the forms speak to them. Believe me, this is not mystical, it is hard work, and the secret to everything in life.

The simple fact is that people who teach by speaking are usually trying to explain what they don't know. They are making up reasons to bolster their lack of understanding, and their reasons are usually wrong. I say this after almost fifty years of watching people teach.

The really sad thing is that they are going to try to explain this article, have a dialogue about it in their head.

What they really need to do is do the forms until all dialogues stop happening in their head.

They need to create silence, first of the voice, then through their forms.

This is the only way to really learn true Karate.

Two Styles of Karate and the Tongbei Solution

The two styles of Karate are Shorei and Shorin. One of the styles of Karate is for large people, and the other is for small people. Another way to look at it is one of the styles of karate is for heavy handed power, and the other is for quick, light people.

To be honest, the distinctions between these two martial arts variations have largely disappeared. This is because, in this writer's opinion, there has been a lack of teacher ability, and a general obsession for power. This has resulted in a loss of the quick footed style, and a degradation of actual power in the heavy footed art.

I first began martial arts in Kenpo, back in the 60s, and the teacher (Rod Martin) was short and light footed. As Kenpo was more intent on hand motion, and less on stances, there was virtually no development of power. Speed, however, was there aplenty. The best teachers had a natural speed.

When I went to the Kang Duk Won I encountered tongbei speed and power. Tongbei refers to internal Kung Fu, much like Tai Chi Chuan, and it had been injected into the Kang Duk Won.

The teacher at this school (Bob Babich) was short and fast. He had the same natural speed, but there was a difference between the two teachers.

The Kenpo teacher was quick and fast, and when he hit you you knew you were hit. Fine and good, what everybody expected from Karate.

The Kang Duk Won teacher had the same quickness and speed, but everything was totally different.

When he moved there was a whiplike motion to him, and you could feel the very air crackle with power.

He was speedy and light, perfect for a light art, but he was injecting Tongbei power into it, internal power.

As I said, the air would crackle with his motion, and when he stomped his foot to emphasize a technique you could feel the floor shake...and the timbers in the building would actually shiver.

Further, he had a sixth sense in everything he did. He would anticipate and move before, seriously before, any attack. He had immaculate control, able to actually touch your eyeball with his finger in the middle of freestyle. Most important, and probably crucial to it all, he was polite.

I know, doesn't seem to fit, but there it was, and it took me decades to figure out the significance here.

He was doing less for more.

He was exerting less and less effort, and getting more and more power.

And this made him not hungry for power, but polite.

When I explain this to people, even quoting The Tao to them (Do nothing until nothing is left undone, etc.), they don't understand.

The large misfortune is that I am large person, over six feet.

I tapped into the tongbei power, but in a different manner than Bob. I can do things, but because of my frame I can't do them the same as Bob, and I have different abilities. It makes it difficult to teach in the same manner as he.

Still, the Tongbei influence is alive and well, just manifesting differently in a different person with a different body.

The good news is that I wrote down many of the pertinent exercises we were doing at the Kang Duk Won.

Some of these had no names, we just did them.

Most of them I have never seen in any other school. They simply don't seem to exist outside the Kang Duk Won of the 60s and 70s, nor in any style of Kung Fu I have seen.

I often wonder if they were a simple invention of the fellow who 'invented' the Kang Duk Won. A fellow name of Joon Byung In. He was at the crux, he learned Kung Fu, then twisted it into the style of Karate he learned.

Well, it is something to wonder about.

Anyway, I wrote down many of these exercises, put them in a book called 'Amazing Fighting Drills.' It is possible to get that tong bei power, which is no longer taught in any style of Karate I have seen, if one reads that book and does the drills listed in it.

The person would have to change his style of Karate, eliminate the obsession for (false) power that has become the hallmark of Karate, but it is possible.

I make no guarantees.

I put that book up for sale, and sold almost no copies.

The problem was probably in my marketing, maybe even in the title itself.

What if I had called it something like, 'Tongbei Fighting Secrets of the Ancient Masters,' or something else like that. Hmmm. I'll have to think further on that.

And, if I was really good at marketing, maybe that would have helped.

I eventually took that book off the market, let it gather dust while I thought about it. Then I put in as a freebie on the course offered at KangDukWon.com.

That's where you'll find it. Three or four belt levels along, in the best online Karate course in the world.

This has been an article about two styles of Karate and the Tongbei Solution.

Taking on the Tough Guys with Karate Training

I was a real drub when I started my Karate Training. A white boy from suburbia. A scaredy cat. I would look at a big, tough, bearded, tattooed guy, and all sorts of alarm bells would go off in my head. Then, I started my karate training at the Kang Duk Won, I met some Hell's Angels and other outlaw biker types, and things changed.

The Kang Duk Won, you see, was filled with gnarly outlaw bikers. There were Gypsy Jokers and Hell's Angels, and all sort of other tough looking fellows. And they all had beards, and tats, and they weighed a lot, and had big muscles, and...they made me nervous.

So training started, and I was paired up with one of these guys, and my nervousness showed, and he looked at me with disdain.

But over time, my nervousness wilted.

I was smashing my forearms against their forearms, trading kicks to the belly, stopping my fist a hair from their noses, and...I got over it. And, I learned one of the most fascinating lessons of my life.

Tattoos are like some kind of mystic armor. People cover themselves with tats because...there is a certain kind of fear within. Something like...they haven't been accepted, so they flaunt their difference, and that is their armor.

And the facial hair, it stops people from looking at their faces, stops people from seeing them, so they can hide.

Do you wear sunglasses? Don't want people to see your eyes, eh? How come? The eyes are the windows to the soul...are you hiding the soul that is you? How come?

Interesting questions, eh? But the point is this: this is why you study the martial arts. You study them so you can get over your nervousness, look your fellow man in the eye, aren't hiding yourself behind anything.

So I stopped being nervous, and the big, hairy, muscular guys accepted me, and I found out something interesting. The big guys wanted friends. They didn't have many, so they wanted, and they were among the most loyal people I have ever met.

Mind you, I never grew beard or got tats, but I managed to hold my own with these guys, and, you know...somehow...they managed to get over their fear of me!

The Black Belt Who Tried to Shut Down Kang Duk Won Karate

Speaking of Black Belts, I once met one who had actually walked into the Kang Duk Won and tried to shut that dojo down.

I met him at the place I worked, a plastics factory in Sunnyvale, when I discovered that he knew Karate.

We talked, and he told me that he had been made a 3rd degree black belt because he could 'fight so good.'

I know he knew one form, the horse stance form, but I don't think he knew any others.

He claimed that he knew the Mu Duk Kwon, or the Oo Duk Kwon, or something like that. It's been a long time, and we only talked about it briefly.

So he had a black belt, and he said that he and his teacher used to go to karate schools, sign up for a free, introductory class, and then pick a fight with the instructor and beat him up.

True.

He named several schools, one of which I knew had gone out of business.

Then he told me about the time he walked into the Kang Duk Won to get a free class and shut it down.

This interested me, because this was my school.

He and his teacher walked in, and were greeted politely. They talked for a few minutes, but the teacher, Bob Babich, didn't say much, and his eyes started squinting, and he started staring at them.

That's it, just getting intense. No warning, 'no howdie do what art ya study,' just...a look. A look that penetrated right through the two fellows.

The two fellows began to feel uneasy, then downright queasy.

This had never happened to them before, and suddenly, the teacher decided they should leave.

After hearing the story I decided to do some checking of my own, so I went to the top black belt, who had actually been described as present at the time of the confrontation. His name was Ron, and he described the incident, without prompting, exactly as the black belts had.

He said that Bob Babich (the owner of the school) had suddenly gotten real tight. Just looked at those two fellows so intently that even Ron wanted to back away. And he was just an onlooker, off to the side.

Now, interestingly, I always remembered that story, and years later I had my own school.

One day this fellow came in, walked up to my partner and started talking.

I saw it a mile away. I saw it in the way the guy was twisting himself for the punch. The way he was mentally setting himself. The way he was edging the conversation.

He fully intended to cold cock my partner.

I moved in from the side and took a position. When he punched I was going to hit him. And I could feel this manic glee, and I had a vision of this fellow flying through the wall and into the accounting office next door.

I was about to tap into my art big time.

He started to move, and I shifted.

He looked at me.

Back to my partner, he started to move, and I started to move.

And this happened a couple more times, and the guy gave it up.

I had split his intention, and destroyed his purpose, simply by understanding it, and moving into it.

Not as good as Bob, but it certainly stopped a fight and saved my partner.

Interesting people, these fake black belts, they think it is about fighting, when it is not about fighting at all.

Finding The True Art in the Kang Duk Won

I look around at the classy dojos these days and I shudder. I see the wall length mirrors and the immaculate rows of bags, and I shudder. These places are nothing like what I experienced at the Kang Duk Won.

The Kang Duk Won was born of a classmate of Gichin Funakoshi's, and therefore it is one of the purest representations of Karate in existence. It was taken to Korea, and treated to that countries harsh winters and boiling summers, all of which made it an art for men to study. Eventually it came to the United States, and I studied it under the tutelage of Bob Babich in San Jose.

Next to the Kang Duk Won was the Towne Theater, which morally defunct cinema had the glory of showing a movie starring a gal name of Linda Lovelace for over two years. Other businesses included bars and sweat shops. In front of the Kang Duk Won, like as not, you would see a score of motorcyles, courtesy of the Hells Angels, Gypsy Jokers, and just about any other Outlaw Biker gang who wanted to learn the real thing.

The front window was cracked and duc taped together. Visitors sat on a picnic bench to watch class. Bob's office was a cubbyhole just big enough for a desk and two chairs, if you didn't open the chairs.

The mat was made out of sailboat canvas, and a big seam ran up the left side of the mat. It was a dirty, filthy thing, and where forms turned you could see strips of duc tape. And it was small, maybe 15 by 25, but classes of 20 and more would work full bore in their pursuit of the art.

In the back hung the bag, and Bob filled it himself, made it extra heavy. He was always taking it down to get it sewn back together, the darned thing looked like Frankenstein's manhood. We used to kick that thing till it bounced, and the whole building would throb and shake.

Now, you might wonder why and how such a place deserves my eternal admiration, and the answer is simple. No excuses, no whining, no bottles of designer water left at the sides of the mat. Just men working, sweating, giving their all, and building an energy indescribable.

I look at modern schools today, with all their amenities, and I shudder, for I don't feel the manic energy, I don't feel the intensity and the comradeship. I don't think I am being old, I am just terrified that when I die, when I come back in another body, I won't find a group of people that are willing to suffer for the True Art. I won't find something, dirty, ragged, gasping for breath, and yet willing to suffuse my soul with the true spirit of the martial arts, I won't find something like the Kang Duk Won.

The Most Polite Man in the World Did Kwon Bup Karate

I want to tell you about the most polite man in the world, and the art he studied, which is called Kwon Bup Karate. I'll tell you a story about a fight he was in in a moment, but first let me tell you that he never, in the seven years I knew him, raised his voice. What makes this really astounding is that he taught all sorts of outlaw bikers, including the Hells Angels, in San Jose in the sixties.

His name was Bob Babich, and he learned Kyokushinkai Karate from Don Buck, who was probably the first westerner to teach that art in the US. He then learned Kang Duk Won Korean Karate from Norman Rha, and this was probably the first time that art was taught in America. He then formulated seven forms on his own, and called them Kwon Bup.

One night he was in a bar with some of his students. Don't judge, things were different then, and it wasn't unusual for guys to go out and test their martial arts in the real world. At any rate, Bob was with a bunch of bikers, and they were downing drinks and laughing and causing an uproar.

Bob, half soused, got in an argument with a cowboy (yes, there were cowboys in San Jose in the sixties, real cowboys), and the fellow drew back his fist and...a Hell's Angel (Walt) picked the cowboy up by the neck and belt and slammed his head into the bar. "I just saved your life, fellow," and Walt placed the cowboy back on his feet. Everybody laughed.

A while later everybody decided to leave. Bob walked across the parking lot, and suddenly changed his mind. Inebriated, he slurred, "I got to go straighten it out with that guy," and he walked back into the bar. The cowboy was watching from the window, and he enlisted the aid of another cowhand, and they stood on either side of the doorway. Bob walked in, and they jumped on him. Bob was short, they were large, and what happened next was...not expected.

Bob twisted his hips, and thrust out his palms, and both cowboys flew through the air. Now, I knew that hip twist, we studied it all the time, I thought it was for...well, I don't know what I thought it was for. Bob, however, had just used it, and he had flung two very large fellows across a bar, and without really hurting them!

He was the most polite man I ever met, even drunk, and he just wanted to get along with people. When push came to shove however, he handled the situation, and still never really hurt anybody. The real blessing is that he left his knowledge in the series of seven forms that I call Kwon Bup Karate.

The Obsession with False Martial Arts Power

The degradation of Martial Arts in America, what I sometimes refer to as False Martial Arts Power, has several causes.

One of the causes is the dumbing down for the instruction of children. Another would be protective gear. Then there's tournaments and commercialism, and so on.

The biggest cause of the failure of Martial Arts, however, I believe has to do with the obsession for Power. The reason I say this is because it tends to infect instructors, and instructors are the door to the future...be it good or bad.

Simply, when a person uses the art to seek power...he loses the art.

Power over others. Power over students. Power to put one above...which puts others under, and thus degrades the art.

The best Karate teacher I ever met was also the politest. In addition, he rarely spoke.

In seven years he said maybe a dozen things to me. Things like, 'A tight fist is a heavy fist,' and 'there are many ways to the top of the mountain,' and, the ever enticing, 'how's work.'

He simply didn't talk. Even on the mat, he would simply say, 'turn your foot,' or 'sink your weight,' or, during incredibly potent demonstrations of power, instead of a kiai he would say, 'Wham!'

Yes. Wham. Unbelievable.

Now I see people giving ornate instructions on bowing eighteen times and the correct angle of the head and the significance of the ancients.

Talk, talk, talk.

And it is all an obsession with power.

Listen to me. I'm saying something important! Listen!

Instead of doing the forms.

Too much talk and not enough work.

When there is less talk, there is more silence, and in silence the lesson can be learned.

When there is less talk the student won't be overwhelmed with words, but able to be struck by a simple sentence, or even just one word.

The desire to talk is a desire to explain, instead of letting the student experience.

The desire to be the 'authority' reveals the weakness that one is NOT the authority, and is relying on talk to disguise that weakness.

The desire to be an authority, to make people listen to you, is an attempt to subjugate people, which is the mark of a teacher in fear.

A teacher who doesn't understand what he is teaching.

A teacher who doesn't understand what he is teaching, and is trying to cover that fact up.

That's what it means in The Tao...no high without low. A description of why a person obsessed with false power puts people under.

A false desire for power over others, by making others listen, subjugating them to words, making yourself an authority.

That best Karate teacher I mentioned? The one who rarely talked? He didn't seek power. He did the art, and power came to him. Real power. Not the false power of admiring masses, but the power of true ability in the martial arts. He knew what people were going to do before they did it. He could touch an eyeball with a finger that could penetrate a board and leave a hole.

He did the art, until the art did him.

Let me bring it home with this loose analogy.

As soon as you care what somebody else is doing...you're a politician.

The alternative is to be a craftsman. An artist.

Not bowing masses, not admiring throngs who have accepted your empty teachings as substance...but a personal self worth that is silent, needs no admiration, and is the human being at his best.

This has been a page about the obsession for false martial arts power.

Real Karate Does Not Look Like Karate!

This concept, that working Karate does not resemble the Karate that people are taught, is actually true throughout the martial arts. Shaolin done in combat does not look like classical wu shu. Kung fu doesn't resemble kung fu, and so on.

The reason for this is that there is pretty, and then there is functional. A fellow teaches, or learns karate, and the instructor shows him something that looks good. Once one starts applying force to the technique, however, the technique must sometimes change to work.

Take a look at the classical wu shu back stance. The stance is so low on the back leg that the ankle is twisted and unable to support the weight of most attacks. Thus, one must change the shape of the form in order to make it work in real life.

Or, take a look at the common middle block in Karate. It swings sideways, and there is no structure, body or real weight behind it.

The correct way to do this block is to shoot it out from the tan tien, which would put the weight and structure behind the thing.
The examples I have just given you, incidentally, represent the reasons why many classical arts fall apart in the Mixed Martial Arts ring. The artists have been trained to look good, and not to make it work. To make something like Karate work in the MMA, or the UFC, one is going to have to change the whole structure of the thing.

Changing the structure of a martial art is not bad, if it makes the art work. Unfortunately, many teachers will scream, and one has to wonder why this is. After all, the fact that an art now works should be proof and satisfaction all in one.

I suppose what is at the heart of some teacher's inability to change is the love of the mystery. What is happening in their minds is that they don't understand what they are doing, but they have become convinced that if they just keep doing what they are doing, they will, eventually, understand it. Thus, they become blind to change, to what works, and, sadly, the potential of the true art.

The good news is that most martial artists I have encountered are willing to change. I show them basic matrixing principles, for instance, and they are glad to change. Thus, hold to the old only so long as it works, change to the new if it doesn't, and watch the True Martial Arts explode across the face of this planet.

Things Wrong With Classical Karate Training

You know, Karate sometimes gets a bad rap these days. You see all the MMA guys trashing their opponents, and you wonder why, if Karate is so good, you don't see it in the octagon. The reason, of course, is the problem with Classical Karate training methods.

In traditional karate classes students are lined up, and they kick and punch and do everything together. This is great, for beginners. The unfortunate fact, however, is that one rapidly progresses from being a beginner, and then needs to have a different teaching method.

Class exercises are fine to warm up, but there is no real exchange of information going on between teacher and student. Oh, you think that everything is in the forms, that you just need to do the forms and enlightenment will burst upon you? Well, true to a certain extent, but there is also the fact that if you hold to this opinion too hard you are saying that karate is for stupid people.

Oh, I'm quite serious when it comes to this. Look, Karate, be it Isshin Ryu or shotokan or uechi ryu or whatever, depends on understanding the physics of the body. And, once a person has understood the first set of physics, there is another set of physics concerning the mind and the spirit. But, because of ancient training methods, methods that were used more to control children than teach artists, nobody in the martial arts really understand what the second set of physics is.

Let me take one example and work with it a bit. I had a student who had terrible form, and he had taken a year of traditional martial arts training. He was terrible, but-smile in the eyes of his sensei-he was very rigid.

So his shoulders overturned, his body was always rotated the wrong way, his punches wouldn't hurt a seven year old girl, but he was deemed good because he was rigid. All his muscles locked into place at the focal point of the technique. And, you can see this same tendency on any number of youtube Karate videos, by any number of 'masters.'

Now, one of the first concepts of real fighting is, 'a sitting duck is a dead duck.' Heck, the reason that gangster told you to hold still when he's talking to you was because he wanted a motionless target. This goes against the true karate somebody would learn if they could get past the stiff, no data teaching that is prevalent in nearly every karate class on the planet.

Real Karate is liquid, and the points of rigidity are so short they shouldn't be perceived, and the karateka is able to move in any direction without preparation or telegraphing. True Karate is a whip, and only the hand tightens, and that momentarily when it smacks through some fool's front teeth. Karate is beauty in motion, not stiff and rigid, and that is just one of the problems with Classical Karate Training.

If you want to learn some great karate, you should head over to my Temple Karate DVD. I've been doing classical karate for over four decades, but I've still got some liquid left in me. There are 11 kata, complete with all the self defense techniques.

The Three Distractions that Stop One
from Reaching the True Martial Art.

There is one thing, and one thing only, that stops a martial artist from achieving his goal in the martial arts. That one thing is termed simple and merely...distraction. To the degree that one is not distracted, to that degree he is successful, and to that degree he achieves the True Art.

When one learns the martial arts one learns these things called forms. On the surface, the form is a method of remembering techniques, of having a curriculum which will teach him higher and higher ranges of art. It is under the surface, however, through the refusal of distractions that one finds the True Martial Art.

When one can refuse to have his attention wander in the middle of form one is cultivating his discipline. When one focuses only on the moves within the form, and does not allow himself to be sidetracked, then he is building concentration. The end result of these endeavors is to be able to keep awareness in the universe of the form, and not in the universe of trees and bushes and rocks and twigs and such.

The pieces of the form, the techniques, are the middle ground of refusing distraction. This area, applying technique to a willing opponent, bridges the perfection of the thought into the perfection of idea even in chaos. When one holds to the physics, holds to his concentration, holds to the truth of his fellow man even in combat, then one is approaching a distraction free existence.

It is in the fact of freestyle, however, that one must find his ultimate refusal of the distractions of the outer world. One must focus on the opponent, refuse the belches and chirps of a random world, and build the truth of his own awareness. When one lives as if in a tunnel with his opponent, and can hold to the construction of that tunnel no matter what, then one is in the True Martial Art.

These three arenas, forms, technique and freestyle, are the arena of the true art. To the extent that one refuses distraction, that one becomes pure and able to hold to concentration and awareness, to this extent one enters the True Martial Art. The real key, to all this, however, lies in the realization of one important factor.

The universe runs backwards. It is not the things of the universe that hold distraction, it is the knowledge that one must not go towards a distraction free existence with effort, but, rather, but relax himself so that no distractions can find purchase in his soul. It is the emptiness of the universe, perceived by the individual free of contention, that is the Truth of the Path of the True Art.

Three Types of Martial Arts Styles When It Comes to Work Outs

Most people when they think of Martial Arts Styles, think of karate versus kung fu, or taekwondo versus Chinese Kenpo. What this article is concerned with, however, are the types of training one goes through to learn martial arts. There three specific routes one can travel down.

The first is the classical martial arts training method. This is going to consist of learning classical karate forms, Kung Fu patterns, and that sort of thing. This is a very intense type of martial arts education.

One has to do the forms endlessly, paying attention to the turn of the foot, the bend of the wrist, making sure the karate stances stay low, and that sort of thing. Some people hold this in disregard, calling for more reality. The truth, however, is that when it comes to martial arts styles of training, it takes a lot of intelligence and focus of attention to do the classical martial arts route.

The second in the martial arts styles of training has to do with focusing on bunkai, or form applications. This is a very heavy self defense regimen, and it works well. One will find this regimen used to great effect in such arts as Judo, Jujitsu, Aikido, and so on.

Of course, how the teacher focuses his training is going to have a large effect. The Jujitsu stylist may tend to be more UFC or MMA oriented, and make his techniques brutal for the street. An Aikido instructor will opt for the spiritual benefits of the martial art.

The last in these martial arts styles of training is to focus on nothing but freestyle. This is the most street ready type of training, and you will find it in Jeet Kune Do, boxing, and other eclectic martial arts. There is a drawback, however, to this type of training.

People who train for the street tend to become trigger happy, a little too excited to use what they have learned. This can cause more fights than it stops. The best option would be to select a school that cushions its hard fighting training with forms and applications.

Forms, Applications, and Freestyle. These are the three corners of the martial arts that will balance the student and keep him safe and learning. When it comes to martial arts styles of training one should always look to a balanced path of learning, for this will keep one safe on the street even as it enhances the spirit.

The Great $2 Karate Lesson!

How much Karate can you learn for $2? Eh?

Well, maybe a lot, especially if you have $2 to spend on the Best Online Karate Lessons in the World.

This Karate Lesson is actually a course, and it takes a person right from white belt through black belt.

The question is...is it worth the money.

Consider the contents of the first karate lesson, the white belt to orange belt level. On that lesson you get a check list to go through. The checklist is thorough.

You get a section on how to do warm ups.

You get a link to a section on Karate basics, all done in video.

You get advice on how to do Martial Arts forms and techniques.

You get a section on how to do the first Karate Kata, or form.

You get a section on how to do the applications so they will REALLY work.

And, you get a BONUS section on how to translate the movements into the methods used by the original founders of the art. This BONUS section itself is worth gold! It takes you back to how and why Karate was invented, and what the original moves had to have been.

And, the thing makes so much sense that you can't argue!

And, even if you are slow to think and do wish to argue, you can't stop thinking about this totally original take on what Karate is!

Now, with this much quantity, and, to be honest, this much quality, why is the price so low?

Because there are a lot of people out there who a) believe you can't trust the net, b) believe that you can't learn the martial arts off the internet, c) believe that the thing is a scam!

But who can argue if it only costs two bucks to find out?

The good news is that this lesson isn't a 'cheapie' to entice to learn and then gouge, it is representative of a sequence of prices that are UNBELIEVABLE!

And, the ulterior motive here?

To teach people good, solid Karate. To make them think, to realize, to get strong and powerful.

To make the weak strong, and the bullies into non-bullies.

And, who knows, you might get to loving this spectacular art so much you order other courses!

Of course, it'll cost you $2 to find out.

Al Case has near 50 years of Martial Arts experience, and was a writer for the Martial Arts Magazines. This course can be found at KangDukWon.com.

About the Author

Al Case walked into his first martial arts school in 1967. During the Gold Age of Martial Arts he studied such arts as Aikido, Wing Chun, Ton Toi Northern Shaolin, Fut Ga Southern Shaolin, Weapons, Tai Chi Chuan, Pa Kua Chang, and others.

In 1981 he began writing for the martial arts magazines, including Inside Karate, Inside Kung Fu, Black Belt, Masters and Styles, and more.

In 1991 he was asked to write his own column in Inside Karate.

Beginning in 2001 he completed the basic studies of Matrixing, a logic approach to the Martial Arts he had been working on for over 30 years.

2011 he was heavily immersed in creating Neutronics, the science behind the science of Matrixing.

Interested martial artists can avail themselves of his research into Matrixing and Neutronics at MonsterMartialArts.com.

DO YOU WANT A LIFETIME OF MARTIAL ARTS NOW?

Or do you want to study for a year or two, lose your zest, forget your lessons so that you can get married, go to school, etc?

If you want a lifetime of martial arts knowledge, then you should start with The Biggest Martial Arts Lesson of All, read a chapter or two every day, and study the martial arts of Al Case at the same time.

Al Case is the inventor of Matrixing, the only real science of the martial arts on the planet.

The Biggest Lesson of All parallels his progression in the martial arts...over a fifty year period.

Here is list of materials to be studied in the recommended order.

BIGGEST LESSON ~ VOLUME ONE ~ original, kenpo, taekwondo, martial arts equipment, karate, Kang Duk Won.

_____ Matrix Karate video course MonsterMartialArts.com
_____ Matrix Karate 5 book series (available on Amazon)
_____ Master Instructor Course MonsterMartialArts.com
_____ Creating Kenpo 3 book series (available on Amazon)
_____ Black Belt video course MonsterMartialArts.com

BIGGEST LESSON ~ VOLUME TWO ~ basics, stances, punches, kicks, odds and ends.

_____ The Punch book MonsterMartialArts.com
Encyclopedia of Karate ~ 5 books
_____ pan gai noon (available through Amazon)
_____ kang duk won karate (available through Amazon)
_____ kwon bup karate (available through Amazon)
_____ outlaw karate (available through Amazon)
_____ buddha crane karate) (available through Amazon)
Videos of some of the above are available at MonsterMartialArts.com

BIGGEST LESSON ~ VOLUME THREE ~ forms, black belt, zen, odds and ends.

_____ Temple Karate book and video at MonsterMartialArts.com

BIGGEST LESSON ~ VOLUME FOUR ~ fighting, weapons, odds and ends.

_____ Matrix Combat book and video at MonsterMartialArts.com
_____ Matrix Kung Fu (Monkey Boxing) book and video at MonsterMartialArts.com
_____ Blinding Steel book and MonsterMartialArts.com

BIGGEST LESSON ~ VOLUME FIVE ~ weapons (cont'd) aikido, crowd walking, kung fu.

_____ shaolin butterfly book and video course MonsterMartialArts.com
_____ Aikido book and video course MonsterMartialArts.com

BIGGEST LESSON ~ VOLUME SIX ~ kung fu (cont'd), masters, pa kua chang, chi power.

_____ butterfly pa kua chang book and video course MonsterMartialArts.com
_____ Matrixing Chi book MonsterMartialArts.com

BIGGEST LESSON ~ VOLUME SEVEN ~ chi power (cont'd) tai chi chuan, other martial arts, yoga, how to teach yourself.

_____ Matrix tai chi chuan video course MonsterMartialArts.com
_____ five army tai chi chuan video course MonsterMartialArts.com
_____ Yoga: The Yoga Kata (book) (available through Amazon)
_____ Black Belt Yoga (book) (available through Amazon)

BIGGEST LESSON ~ VOLUME EIGHT ~ how to teach yourself (cont'd), mysticism, how to teach the martial arts, matrixing.

_____ Create Your Own Art book and video course
_____ How to Start Your Own Martial Arts School (book) (available through Amazon)

BIGGEST LESSON ~ VOLUME NINE ~ matrixing (cont'd), neutronics, odds and ends.

_____ Matrixing: The Master Text (book) MonsterMartialArts.com
_____ How to Matrix the Martial Arts (available through Amazon)
_____ Neutronics: Prologue and Neutronics (book) (available through Amazon)
_____ Neutronics: The Neutronic Viewpoint and The 24 Principles (book) (available through Amazon)
_____ The Science of Matrixing in the Martial Arts (available through Amazon)
_____ Matrixing Tong Bei book (available through Amazon)
_____ Binary Matrixing (available through Amazon)

BIGGEST LESSON ~ VOLUME TEN ~ odds and ends

_____ The Master Books MonsterMartialArts.com

_____ Matrixing Jeet Kune Do book (available through Amazon)

_____ Fixing MCMAP book (available through Amazon)

_____ Neutropia (poetry book) (available through Amazon)

_____ The Bodyguard Training Manual (book) (available through Amazon)

_____ Monkey Boxing Forms (book) (available through Amazon)

_____ Karate to Shaolin to Pa Kua Chang (book) (available through Amazon)

_____ 3rd Level 6th Sense Swordfighting (book) (available through Amazon)

_____ How to Matrix Kick Boxing (book) (available through Amazon)

NOVELS BY AL CASE

Many of these novels have martial arts sub-themes intwined in them.

MACHINA SERIES
The Haunting of House
Machina (two parts)

MONKEYLAND SERIES
Monkeyland
The Bomber's Story (two parts)
The Lone Star Revolt
Yancy (part of Yancy series)
Return to Monkeyland

ASSASSIN SERIES
Hero
Assassin
Avatar

YANCY SERIES
Small in the Saddle
When the Cold Wind Blows
When the Black Dog Dies
Yancy (part of Monkeyland series)

WIZARD OF PARTS SERIES
The Path of the Snake
The Path of the Wizard
The Path of the Dragon

LOBO LOVE SERIES
Lobo Love
Werewolf University

STANDALONE BOOKS
The Day the President Killed the United States
The Day They Bombed the Hell Out of Los Angeles
Twisted Gods
Falling Skies
Pack
The Party from Hell
The Ethereal Bodyguard
How to Kill
The North Mansion
The Transformation of George Cogswell
The Light of the Lunatic Yogi's Eyeballs

OTHER BOOKS
How to Write: Blood and Ink
The Simple Truth About Algebra
How to Create Your Own Secret Language (Pig Latin)